SIX LIES PEOPLE BELIEVE ABOUT DIVINE HEALING

THE TRUTH ABOUT GOD'S WILL TO HEAL THE SICK

STEVE BREMNER

Illustrated by
JOSE ALJOVIN

It is rare to find a perfect book, but in this day and age of digital books and print-on-demand publishing, we can correct our mistakes rather quickly. If you find a typo or error in this book, we'd be extremely grateful if you would drop us an email to let us know.

Contact us at fireonyourhead@stevebremner.com

ACKNOWLEDGMENTS

None.

Who uses the word "acknowledgment" anyway? I prefer thank you's or 'shout-outs'

I felt it would be inappropriate not to include a moment to give thanks to the many friends and volunteers who helped make this book what it is today. As such, I will not be able to thank *every* single individual who could be thanked for this project coming together, and hope anybody who expected to see their name here is not offended that I left it out. There are just simply too many to list and thank personally.

In writing a book on divine healing, it would be criminal of me not to personally thank Brian Parkman for all the seeds he planted in my spirit on this subject in both Bible college and in personal Skype calls over the years. If it weren't for you Brian, I never would have taken this journey. Much of what I've taught others and written in this book would never have come about. As I penned many of these thoughts, both on my blog over the years and recently into the book, I could hear your voice and passion coming through ideas I've learned from you.

As I re-read that last sentence, it does sound kind of creepy, I realize.

I also thank Joel Crumpton, not only for teaching me a lot of this stuff as well, but for helping me put it into practice on the streets of Charlotte while I was in FIRE School of Ministry. Also kudos for believing in my podcast and being willing to come on it regularly over the years to share testimonies and stir others up to deliver healing to those who need it. May this book have the same effect as those discussions with you have had on thousands. I owe much of what I believe and live out to you and Brian, two great men of God.

I also want to thank those of you who've encouraged my writing gift and made me think "why not?" when it comes to publishing a work such as this, of which this will be the first of many more books.

Of course, I've had many volunteers and personal friends proofread and review the manuscript in various stages and to each of you I'm eternally grateful. I want to thank Kathryn Hughey for being the first to respond and get back to me with constructive feedback when I announced on social media that I was looking proofreaders. But I *especially* need to thank Sharon Toh, for your exceptional editorial and proofreading skills that have helped take the quality of this project to a whole other level that I never could have reached on my own. May God bless you with MANY other authors hiring you to edit their projects!

Special thanks to Jose Aljovin for the cover, and all the artwork related to the book and promotional images. You've got great taste and insight.

And I want to thank my wife-to-be, Lili, for being willing to be my wife. I merely wanted to mention your name in my first book. Te quiero mucho, baby!

Finally, I obviously don't want to leave out my Lord and Savior Jesus Christ, Who was and is and always will be the Passover Lamb by Whose stripes we are healed.

Sharing and lending this book is highly encouraged. I'd love it if you had your friends buy it, but more importantly, I would love it if your friends stopped believing lies and got healed. I'd love it even more if you laid your hands on the sick and saw them get healed.

One night in August 2004, Billy Burke, a minister from Tampa, Florida was in my hometown of Peterborough, Ontario. He had been coming almost every month for a Friday night healing meeting followed by a Saturday morning teaching seminar. I had persuaded my mom, a pharmacist who works in several different nursing homes to come to that month's Friday night meeting. She had been suffering from fibromyalgia for as long as I could remember. She couldn't really do much without feeling tired and she always needed to be sitting or lying down. She always seemed to be in pain.

When worship started in the service, I noticed she was very enthusiastic about it — raising her hands and everything. This was not only uncharacteristic of her, but we didn't do that kind of stuff at the church we came from. I knew something was up with her, as I had never seen her this way in church before.

After Billy Burke preached and shared a lot of testimonies to boost everyone's faith, he started calling people out of the audience who needed healing. We watched a blind woman be led onto the stage and he prayed for her until she told him how many fingers he was holding up. People were removing their hearing aids and plugging their other ear — repeating what he whispered to them. One woman unplugged her oxygen tank after receiving prayer and I didn't see her plug it back in for the rest of the night. If memory serves me correctly, she also had a knee injury or something too. She proclaimed that she could breathe and walk. She was totally freed from a lung condition she had prior to attending the service. It was powerful and memorable!

My mom turned to me after all of this and asked if she could go up to the front to get prayer as well. I said, "Sure." I went with her and at least 45 minutes went by while Burke prayed for people and the church's ushers and "catchers" helped gently let people down to the floor as they fell under the power of God. We had to keep stepping aside in order to not trip on the people while others ran around us to prove they could really walk again.

Finally, he announced that instead of praying individually at length with each person, he'd just lay hands on people because it was getting late and there were still a lot of people in the altar area waiting for a healing miracle. When he laid hands on my mom, I thought she was going to pass out. That would have made me laugh — because again, I'd never seen her as excited as she was that night around the "crazy charismatics". She did not fall down, but she later told me she was so "woozy" that she needed to sit down — woozy in a good way that she had never felt before.

We sat down and she began filling out a "testimony card" that an usher had offered her. She shared her doubts about filling it out with the usher – explaining to him that she knew she was healed the instant she walked into the building. She had previously been in so much pain that she couldn't lift her arms up. Remember I told you a moment ago that I knew something was up when she was worshipping so passionately during the praise time? That was why.

We decided to go over to where a friend's parents were sitting to say hello, and specifically to tell them about my mom's healing. She told them something that she had neglected to tell me: that on that particular day, her painkillers had run out and she purposely didn't renew them because she knew God wanted to heal her and *would* do so that night. Up to that point, I did not know that particular detail.

My mom had fibromyalgia for close to 15 years. Over the following weekend, I heard her tell other people a lie that she had believed for the majority of that period. Her view of God was that if you had something wrong with you — such as a disease or illness, then it was wrong and impolite to ask God to remove it. She erroneously believed — like many Christians do — that God puts sickness and burdens on people to teach them a lesson. She believed this lie for years, but was willing to challenge it — thanks to a conversation that I honestly cannot remember having with her. On an occasion prior to that healing service, I had asked her to show me in the Bible where God makes people ill. Since there is no such example in the Word of God — only so in a man-made teaching, apparently the question I posed settled it for her and she agreed to come to the meeting.

The weekend my mom got healed, I sent out a testimony e-mail to my entire e-mail list to testify to what God had done. By that time, I was already on fire to see more miraculous healing in my life and ministry, and I wanted to encourage others. Something weird happened. Instead of being happy that God had done this for my mom, I encountered a lot of resistance from Christians. Many of them believed lies such as these that I intend to dismantle in this book. As a result, a fire was lit in me to start researching the Scriptures more in order to help prove that divine healing is for today and not just something in the Bible days.

I started a blog and re-wrote the original e-mail for my first post. I originally intended on making the focus of the blog healing and planned to share weekly testimonies as I went on the streets of downtown Charlotte, North Carolina, with other Bible college students that Fall. Eventually, I blogged about all sorts of things, especially providing solid Bible foundation for various "charismatic" doctrines and topics.

I couldn't help but think "What if my mom had that lie destroyed much earlier?" She could have saved herself fifteen years of pain in her physical body. Then I realized what if I believed lies that were holding me back? Wouldn't I want someone to open my eyes?

That brings us to the purpose of this book. It is an attempt at opening the eyes of those who need their eyes to be opened. For those whose eyes are already open, this book will serve as an opportunity to be encouraged and strengthened in the truth about God's will to heal.

WHY ARE YOU READING THIS BOOK?

I want to thank you for opening this book, whether you purchased it or obtained it some other way. Before you begin reading further, I want to ask you *why* have you chosen to read it? The title is, *"Lies People Believe About Divine Healing"*. Not truths, but lies. If you're like me, you don't want to believe lies. You want the truth.

Well, you're in luck. I've provided you some of the top lies people believe about divine healing, and proceed to dismantle them and go into our main source of insight for the truth: the Scriptures themselves. Whether you believe that divine healing is for today or not, the Bible has much to say on the subject. Unfortunately, some have fallen for the half truths and misinformation out there.

This book is for readers who no longer want to be held back. The point is not only to dismantle a number of strongholds and draw attention to lies, but to replace them with facts. And not just facts, truths. Our standard of truth is the Word of God.

By no means do I count myself an expert on divine healing, because frankly, the *whole* Body of Christ should be manifesting His presence seeing people healed, set free, delivered, saved — or whatever term you want to use — it encompasses the whole person — and is not just something special "healing experts" do. But that's just the point — it's *natural* to me. I want it to be natural to you too. It's natural to a lot of my Christian friends.

There are larger and larger cultures within the Body of Christ that are embracing a supernatural lifestyle. I believe those with healing gifts who are healing stadiums full of the sick or injured brought in by the busloads are coming to an end. More and more of the Body of Christ are realizing that as the Head does it, so does the whole Body. Healing is not just for a few gifted ones. In fact, I think those days may already be over and something has shifted. We're seeing the fruit of that throughout many sectors of the Body of Christ.

THE WORD OF GOD IS FOREVER SETTLED

Before proceeding in the direction I'd like to take us in, let's take a look at a few things about the Word of God. It is forever settled in heaven (Ps 119:89-92), therefore it is also forever settled on the earth (Matt 6:10) when it is acted on and enforced. According to Psalm 119:142, it will never change — it is everlasting. What God said thousands of years ago will still be true thousands of years from now. Isaiah 55:11 states that God's Word goes forth and doesn't return void, but accomplishes what it is supposed to do.

I've heard Rev. Curry Blake teach in his *Divine Healing Technician* audio series something like the following; Science has determined that the smallest known particle is that of light, but has also determined that the particle is composed of two smaller components, which is believed to be what we would call sounds, or waves.

Is it possible then that these components are indeed sounds, and they are the words the Lord spoke in creation when he said, "Let there be light"? Genesis 1:3 states that the Lord spoke light into existence. The original Hebrew literally would translate as "Light, be!" Hebrews 11:3 and 2 Peter 3:5 further state that with the [spoken] word of God the universe was created.

Science also tells us that the universe is continuing to expand in every direction. It's my opinion that if man were to go to the very edge of the universe past the point where light has reached so far — there would come a time where you'd experience a wall of light passing around you as it traveled to that point, and in that moment you'd hear the Lord saying, "Light, be!" God's word, though spoken once, is settled forever and is still going forth. However, God doesn't get up every morning and "re-tell" the light to come out upon the earth. He doesn't tell the earth to go around the sun again. It's happening just as He once spoke it to. As Christians, we enforce and establish His will and what He has spoken every time we preach it, cast a demon out on the authority of that Word, heal the sick, and so on.

THE LIGHT SHINES IN THE MIDST OF DARKNESS

> *"The earth was without form and void, and darkness was over the face of the deep. And the Spirit of God was hovering over the face of the waters. And God said, "let there be light," and there was light."* (Gen 1:2-3)

Notice how the Holy Spirit of God was hovering over the darkness, but didn't do anything until the Lord *spoke*. We know from New Testament Scripture that by Christ, all things were created in heaven and on earth, visible and invisible (Col 1:16) — yet the Son is not mentioned in Genesis by name or role. But the opening verses of John elaborate more:

*In the beginning was the Word, and the Word was with God, and **the Word was God**. He was in the beginning with God. All things were made through him, and without him was not any thing made that was made. In him was life, and the life was the light of men. **The light shines in the darkness**, and the darkness has not overcome it.* (John 1:1-5, emphasis mine)

John later quotes Jesus in chapter 9:4: *"We must work the works of him who sent Me while it is day; night is coming when no one can work."* Jesus, full of the Holy Spirit, would do the mighty works of the Lord such as: miracles, healing the sick, and setting the captives free. Jesus would do the work that He saw the Father doing (John 5:19-20). He did the will of the Father, but it is the role of the Spirit to carry it out.

When His captors came to arrest Him, Jesus stated in Luke 22:53, "this is your hour, when darkness reigns." Until His crucifixion, darkness reigned.

We can see moments in the Gospels where the Holy Spirit hovered over the darkness until God's will was declared and spoke forth what the Spirit was to administer. He didn't raise Jesus up a moment earlier than planned, but yet the Holy Spirit was still there hovering over the tomb.

THE SPIRIT FOLLOWS THE WORD

> *"When the Spirit of truth comes, He will guide you into all the truth, for He will not speak on his own authority, but whatever He hears he will speak, and He will declare to you the things that are to come. He will glorify me, for He will take what is mine and declare it to you. All that the Father has is mine; therefore I said that He will take what is mine and declare it to you."* (John 16:13-15)

Jesus told his disciples in John 16:7 that it was a *good* thing that He ascend to heaven, because if He didn't the Holy Spirit–the helper–would not come. This is because prior to Jesus' death and resurrection the Spirit only showed up and moved where Jesus, the Word, was. Now, He the Spirit is indwelling a whole people! From just a numerical and practical standpoint, a large group of people who demonstrate the power of the Gospel, and who do the works Jesus did is exponentially greater than just one man doing them. Until the day of Pentecost there was no Holy Spirit in the world except when and where the Word was preached by Jesus. Then, in the second chapter of Acts, after the upper room experience, Peter was the first man endowed with the Spirit to preach the Gospel message to any hearer. As a result, a large number of people were saved and added to the collective Body of Christ.

Most of the Church gets the role of the Spirit back-wards. We wait to do things until we have some special feeling or validation as to what God's will is and call that "being led by the Spirit." However, most Christians fail to realize calling it "being led by the Spirit" is just spiritual-izing their own laziness, because we're not actually told to "be led by the Spirit"–this idea is taken from only one Scripture verse in the New Testament (Romans 8:14) that many are taking out of context when they quote it. The verse merely says "For all who are led by the Spirit of God are sons of God." This is not a command, but is talking about being led into mortification as opposed to just general leadership.

Scripture tells us to have the mind of Christ (1 Cor 2:16), and to let the Word of Christ dwell in us richly (Col 3:16). It is from this standpoint that we will proceed and use the Word of God to demolish the lies people believe, and replace them with the truth. For what purpose? So that you may help set people free and live free yourself.

The Holy Spirit accompanies the Word and bears witness with it; Mark 16:17-18 states that signs (miracles) would accompany (read FOLLOW) them that believed, not the other way around like most of us think. The Holy Spirit helps YOU, you don't help Him. It would be cliché to say that many charismatics are chasing after signs and wonders, chasing after moves of God when those rivers of living water are actually springing out of us (John 7:37 39)! These rivers of living water already aid us as we preach and proclaim the Gospel. We just need a mind renewal, and I'm hoping you'll allow me to help.

The power of God is intended to be a proof that the Gospel is true. It's supposed to be a means to an end, not the end itself. For example, we do not get excited about a sign that says "50 Miles to Disneyland", as that sign only serves to confirm we are heading in the right direction. We get excited when we *arrive* at Disneyland.

THE SPIRIT AS OUR HELPER

One thing I like to do when teaching on divine healing is to have a volunteer or my interpreter play the role of my 'helper' and act out that I'm a painter or carpenter or some similar profession. A helper in this context is not someone who does the work, but helps the one doing the job. A helper, for our intents and purposes, would be like an apprentice or a handy man. If this helper is a good worker he'll know to anticipate what tools I'll need ahead of time. If I'm standing on a ladder he may be holding my tools for me, anticipating what tool I'm going to need next, and providing it for me before I even have to ask for it. He follows me and gives me what I need to get the job done. However, the Holy Spirit is God Himself and not any less than the Father or the Son. The Spirit deserves our utmost respect and reverence all the same. He is in this role of a helper to the Bride of Christ, the Church. The Holy Spirit knows exactly what is needed in a particular moment or situation, and pulls out of His tool belt either the healing, prophetic Word, knowledge of Scripture, or whatever you need to help you proclaim and advance God's kingdom in the moment.

Remember when Ezekiel spoke to the dry bones: the Spirit acted and did the work. Ezekiel didn't wait for the Spirit to move first, and then "follow" or be "led" by the Spirit and verbally repeat the obvious. He spoke the words of God, and the Holy Spirit energized and activated them. He spoke, and the Spirit of God brought the life – He created living organisms afresh as the bones connected, and flesh appeared on them and created a new living army! But alas, the Holy Spirit can only confirm HIS word, not our ideas or opinions and certainly not our bad theology.

Take note of how Job's friends waxed eloquent and told him all sorts of pious theological-sounding words about why he was going through the trials he was going through. But when Elihu spoke the truth, God showed up in power and spoke to them! Likewise, the Holy Spirit can't anoint something that's not true — He can only agree with the Word. This is why there are so many "dead churches" preaching a Gospel message limited to salvation, and getting what they preach for. Since they don't believe in, preach or teach in the power of God or miracles, consequently they don't see them either.

In his book, *Holy Spirit, Revelation and Revolution: Exploring Holy Spirit Dimensions*, Reinhard Bonnke says:

> *"Prayer is not enough to rouse a dead church. It needs the power of the Word imbued with the life of the Spirit. Life comes from the living Word. What we can do and what we should do is preach the Word. Praying for God to work is fine, but praying for Him to do what we should be doing is pointless. We cannot send his Spirit anywhere. He moves with us, and He is where we are. We cannot pray for God to save souls and bless people and then wait for something to happen. He sends us with the Word and the Spirit awaits us. It is our privilege to work for him, save souls for him. For anyone who thinks they do not have strength or power, the Word is their strength and their power. There are two important things to note: Holy Spirit meetings without the Word are human meetings, and prayer is not a substitute for the Word."* [1]

The Spirit answers prayer in the name of Jesus because He *is* the Word. As Bonnke goes on to phrase it, "The will of the Father is written and is spoken by the Son, the Word, and performed by the Spirit."

> *"Truly, truly, I say to you, whoever hears my word and believes Him who sent me has eternal life. He does not come into judgment, but has passed from death to life."*

*It is the Spirit who gives life; the flesh is no help at
all. The words that I have spoken to you are spirit
and life.*

(John 5:24, 6:63)

Allow me to encourage you to let the Word dwell richly in
you (Colossians 3:16).

We will begin now to establish ourselves in what the
Word of God says on the subject. I have summarized the
most common misconceptions and hindrances people
have regarding God's will to heal them, and I present to
you the following in no particular order.

First, though, allow me to say that in no way am I trying to
be insensitive if you're reading this and are sick yourself,
know someone who is, or have lost a loved one and
reading me just talking about God's favor and supernatural power is striking a chord with you as you read this.

The following book does not address in detail every single
point that it could, but I believe this will whet your
appetite as many others have gone before us and
contributed mightily to the Church in this area. The
books that have most shaped my life and I encourage the
reader to get a hold of are *Healing the Sick* by T.L.
Osborn, and *Christ the Healer*, by F.F. Bosworth. I also
encourage getting a hold of material by John G. Lake.

And now, on with some fuel for your fire and some truths

to stir you up with a strong foundation in regard to faith and healing.

Note

1. Reinhard Bonnke, Holy Spirit Revelation & Revolution: Exploring Holy Spirit Dimensions (Orlando, E-R Productions LLC, 2007)

LIE #1: "IT'S NOT GOD'S TIME"

TO THIS LIE I can't help but ask: when *is* God's time? This deception also sounds pious and religious, but is usually stated by people who are seeking healing in their body but haven't obtained it yet. Or, they gave up before receiving the miracle. Nowhere in Scripture do we find that God withholds the healing until a certain vague and other, nebulous and unquantifiable time has arrived. Healing is a part of the atonement on the cross, and if today is the day of salvation (2 Corinthians 6:2), then today is also the day for healing (salvation of a physical body). What Christ accomplished on the cross has already happened in the past and there is no more "future" tense to it. What's done is done.

In the meantime, notice that in His ministry Jesus healed people spontaneously in Matthew 14:14, where it says

> When He went ashore He saw a great crowd, and He had compassion on them and healed their sick.

Notice it was compassion that caused Him to heal the sick when He came across them here, not timing.

Also, recall with me the passage of the lame man at the pool of Bethesda in John's Gospel,

> In these lay a great multitude of sick people, blind, lame, paralyzed, waiting for the moving of the water. For an angel went down at a certain time into the pool and stirred up the water; then whoever stepped in first, after the stirring of the water, was made well of whatever disease he had. (John 5:3-4, NKJV)

Some observations we cannot escape:

- God did not determine *who* got healed nor when they got healed
- God did not determine the time a person got healed.
- God did not determine that some people should keep their illness until they had learned something (There goes the "God's teaching me a lesson" lie).

HEALING IN THE ATONEMENT OF JESUS CHRIST

Here is a quick overview of healing in the Word of God through the atonement of Jesus Christ. The Scriptures say in Isaiah 53:4-5:

> *"Surely He took up our infirmities and carried our sorrows, yet we considered Him stricken by God, smitten by Him, and afflicted. But He was pierced for our transgressions, He was crushed for our iniquities; the punishment that brought us peace was upon Him, and by his wounds we are healed."*

Christ died for both our sins and our sicknesses. Matthew 8:17 also says this. The concept of health and salvation is littered throughout both testaments. Deuteronomy 28 underscores the curses Israel would receive for their disobedience to God, and the blessings, including health and prosperity, if they'd obey. The Passover lamb in Exodus 15 was both eaten (giving them strength for their

journey) and blood placed over their doorposts to keep
them from the judgment God was bringing on the
Egyptian firstborns.

> *"Praise the LORD, O my soul, and forget not all His
> benefits, who forgives all your sins and heals all your
> diseases."* Psalm 103:3

Also, at the Lord's table we both eat His flesh and drink
His blood. By his stripes (on his body) we are healed, by
His blood we are saved (from judgment, a type of Passover
concept). This is underscored pretty clearly in 1
Corinthians 10:16:

> *"Is not the cup of thanksgiving for which we give thanks a
> participation in the blood of Christ? And is not the bread
> that we break a participation in the body of Christ?"*

Paul goes on to say in chapter 11 of this book

> *"Therefore, whoever eats the bread or drinks the cup of the
> Lord in an unworthy manner will be guilty of sinning
> against the body and blood of the Lord. A man ought to
> examine himself before he eats of the bread and drinks of
> the cup. For anyone who eats and drinks without
> recognizing the body of the Lord eats and drinks
> judgment on himself. That is why many among you are
> weak and sick, and a number of you have fallen asleep.
> But if we judged ourselves, we would not come under*

judgment. When we are judged by the Lord, we are being disciplined so that we will not be condemned with the world."

There are two different things happening here: one pertaining to health and healing the other, salvation. Both are being remembered. This is underscored by how doing it improperly brought about getting sick and weak, and falling asleep (dying). It's unclear to the author if the falling asleep is due to judgment in terms of salvation or the consequences of bad health (not being healed), but at any rate, it was pretty serious and worth paying careful attention to.

Also, Jesus told the man who was lowered through a roof on a mat that he was healed *and* that his sins were forgiven (Luke 5:18-25). And in James 5:15-16,

> *"And the prayer offered in faith will make the sick person well; the Lord will raise him up. If he has sinned, he will be forgiven. Therefore confess your sins to each other and pray for each other so that you may be healed. The prayer of a righteous man is powerful and effective."*

James doesn't say the prayer offered in faith will sometimes maybe make the sick person well. It doesn't say the Lord *might* in certain circumstances raise him up. It says He *will*.

Even throughout the New Testament the concept of

forgiveness of sins and healing of diseases is understood to be part of the same act of redemption on the cross.

The Greek word *sozo* for saved has to do with *complete* salvation, including healing of the body.

Here are few instances of it being translated as "healed":

- Jairus and his daughter: *"My little daughter is dying. Please come and put your hands on her so that she will be **healed** and live."* (Mark 5:23)
- The woman with the issue of blood: *"When she heard about Jesus, she came up behind him in the crowd and touched his cloak, because she thought, "If I just touch his clothes, I will be **healed**."* Mark 5:28
- *"And wherever he went — into villages, towns or countryside — they placed the sick in the marketplaces. They begged him to let them touch even the edge of his cloak, and all who touched him were **healed**."* Mark 6:56 NIV. Note the King James says "made whole".

Here are a few instances of *sozo* being translated "saved":

- The parable of the sower: *"Those along the path are the ones who hear, and then the devil comes and takes away the word from their hearts, so that they may not believe and be **saved**."* Luke 8:12

- *"I am the gate, anyone who enters through me will be **saved**."* John 10:9
- *"For it is by grace you have been **saved**, through faith — and this not from yourselves, it is the gift of God"* Ephesians 2:8
- *"But women will be **saved** through childbearing — if they continue in faith, love and holiness with propriety."* 1 Tim 2:15. I include this example to show that obviously Paul isn't saying women receive salvation by childbearing. However, this instance is an interesting translation into English, able to underscore how interchangeable the concept of physical wholeness (healing/health) and spiritual wholeness (salvation) have the exact same word in the original Greek.

I don't see how, if God is not willing that any should perish (not come to salvation, 2 Peter 3:9), that for some strange reason He'd feel differently about people receiving physical healing since He paid for it in the same act of atonement. It's not that God doesn't save someone, it's because someone doesn't receive it or they reject it. It's not that God doesn't heal people, it's that someone doesn't receive it, or they can choose to reject that God would or will heal them. If he paid for it on the cross, then He doesn't hold out on anyone that needs healing. If people were not getting healed even though God is a Healing God in fact that's one of His names Jehovah Raphe, the

Lord our Healer! Do you think He'd be living up to His word and His name if He didn't always heal? We'd have to call Him "Sometimes He heals" or something more appropriate. This is not the case, He is who He says He is. That people are not getting healed doesn't change God's nature any more than people not getting saved meaning that God doesn't really save people. He died on the cross, it's been paid for and it's up to the recipient to receive healing/salvation.

IF HEALING IS PROVIDED FOR IN THE ATONEMENT, THEN...

...do we have any right to believe everyone who gets saved will automatically get healed when they are saved?

...does God make a distinction between healing the inner man and healing the outer man?

These are good questions.

Faith needs to be built up in the hearts of the hearers. Faith can only be had where the will of God is known. That is why it is necessary to know God's will, as revealed in the Scriptures. That is why this part of the book will not cover everything there is to cover on this subject. I strongly want to encourage you or anyone struggling with the idea that it IS God's will to heal all, to read all the Scriptures in this book and meditate on Scriptures concerning healing. The purpose of this is to bring your faith to a certainty as to what God's will on the matter is. Otherwise these truths will just be a bunch of theological opinions to you, and I doubt you'd benefit from it.

I once heard that Kenneth Hagin said in later years of his ministry that he was seeing far fewer dramatic healings than in his earlier years of ministry. He believed this was the result of teaching only one night and taking less time on the subject before praying for people, as opposed to the days when he'd spend no less than three weeks in the same place teaching on it and building believers up on this subject. So even if, and when, I am being redundant, it's for the specific purpose of hoping to make things clear and understandable. The reason I've chosen to build on this aspect of God's Word that is already forever settled is to build upon foundational things first before establishing other things on top of these truths.

JESUS, SAVIOR OF ALL—INCLUDING OUR BODIES

When we think of Jesus as "Savior", we think in spiritual terms and don't give much thought to what else that also implies. When someone is drowning and asks to be saved, they mean they want to be saved from drowning. In the West, we've made salvation exclusively spiritual. "Saved" has become some kind of term that guarantees people a way into heaven no matter how they live their lives.

The Greek word "sozo" means: to save; to preserve from harm; to keep; to rescue.

When Peter was sinking into the waters he cried out, "Lord save me!" (Matthew 14:30), it was a physical rescue from danger he sought, and he received it. Luke 7:50 records Jesus forgiving the sins of a woman who lived an adulterous life and says "your faith has *sozo*-ed you." In Luke 8:48, Jesus heals the woman with the issue of blood, and tells her "your faith has *sozo*-ed you." Sin and sickness are both forms of death, and Jesus delivers and saves from both. The same way one woman's faith forgave her of her sins, the other woman's faith healed her of her issue of blood. In Luke 8:50, Jesus told Jairus not to fear but only believe and his daughter would be made well (*sozo*). This turned out to be a dead-raising, not a healing, but the same concept is applied and the same word is used.

Jesus is the Savior and He encompassed all these things in the Gospel accounts. The Gospel distinguishes in the New Testament, but it never separates healing from saving. See the prayer of faith in James 5 for example.

Jesus told his disciples to go heal the sick, cast out demons, and preach the Gospel. Do you really think that was just for a special period, and that now, after the New Testament was written, preaching the Gospel of salvation in Christ would no longer include those things that it did in the Gospel accounts? Why wouldn't it?

Jesus saves. However, He saves people from what they need to be saved from. Asking if healing is a part of salvation is like asking if reconciliation is part of forgiveness, or if redemption is a part of salvation. Of course they are, and you can't have one without the other. Redemption has everything to do with restoration. It would not be restoration if we were not restored. This cannot, by definition, only apply to having sins forgiven but being restored as well — spiritually, emotionally, mentally, physically, in every way there is to be restored.

The instant one of us repents and receives salvation we have become born from above, and children of God. It is therefore a legitimate question to ask, "If I have been born from above and my sins are forgiven, then how come I haven't been healed yet?"

Let's look carefully at one of the key texts commonly used to teach that healing is provided for in the atonement and clarify some "sacred cows" and misunderstandings.

1 Who has believed what He has heard from us?

And to whom has the arm of the Lord been revealed?

2 For He grew up before Him like a young plant,

and like a root out of dry ground;

He had no form or majesty that we should look at Him,

and no beauty that we should desire Him.

3 He was despised and rejected by men;

a Man of sorrows, and acquainted with grief;

and as one from whom men hide their faces

> *He was despised, and we esteemed Him not.*

4 *Surely He has borne our griefs*

> *and carried our sorrows;*

yet we esteemed Him stricken,

> *smitten by God, and afflicted.*

5 *But He was pierced for our transgressions;*

> *He was crushed for our iniquities;*

upon Him was the chastisement that brought us peace,

> *and with His wounds we are healed.*

6 *All we like sheep have gone astray;*

> *we have turned—every one—to his own way;*

and the Lord has laid on Him

> *the iniquity of us all.*

7 *He was oppressed, and He was afflicted,*

> *yet He opened not his mouth;*

like a lamb that is led to the slaughter,

> *and like a sheep that before its shearers is silent,*

so He opened not his mouth.

8 *By oppression and judgment He was taken away;*

and as for his generation, who considered

that He was cut off out of the land of the living,

stricken for the transgression of my people?

9 *And they made His grave with the wicked*

and with a rich man in His death,

although He had done no violence,

and there was no deceit in His mouth. (Isaiah 53:1-9)

The idea that Jesus' body was whipped for our sicknesses and that His blood was spilled for our sins — as if they are two separate things, with two separate goals is a false interpretation of the passage. This is a false interpretation because it makes an artificial distinction between the two aspects of redemption, one from sicknesses and the other from sins.

Most Bible translations get away from the fact that in the Hebrew Isaiah 53:4 talks of Jesus bearing our sins and our pains. The Hebrew word used here for "griefs" in most translations, comes from the root word for "maladies" and "diseases" (*"choliy"*, H 2483).

For our purposes, let's compare two views about this that are widely held in Evangelical circles.

View A: Matthew made his own translation of this passage when he brought out the differentiation of "diseases" from iniquities, to make his point in his own writing. Matthew 8:17 is like "Holy Ghost commentary" on the passage in Isaiah 53.

View B: 1 Peter 2:24 is used to say this gives a picture of Jesus' earthly ministry, but then He was nailed to the cross and died for our sins. However, this verse has nothing to do with physical healing, therefore we have no reason to believe for healing through the atonement.

One problem this raises is that Matthew is quoting Isaiah in reference to the healing ministry of Jesus — the context of Jesus healing Peter's mother-in-law. If Isaiah was not talking about or including healing being in the atonement Matthew wouldn't have made this reference the way he did and say Jesus was fulfilling that passage *by* healing. View A says Jesus did both and fulfilled that passage. While view B says "yes of course" Jesus did fulfill this stuff by His earthly ministry, but that was only applicable until He died on the cross and now it's only spiritual healing we receive from His atonement.

Another problem this raises is Isaiah 53 is not either/or with physical & spiritual healing, but both/and. The healing is included in the salvation. The passage describes both/and, therefore our interpretation of it cannot be either/or. When it says in this passage "we esteemed Him stricken", who is the "we" in that sentence? If it applies to us, the New Testament believers, then when did we ever believe He was suffering for his own sins? This then has to be referring to the cross and not Jesus' earthly ministry alone. Since the "we" Isaiah would be writing to was his own people, Israel, then we need to take into account that all those involved in handing Jesus over to be crucified were the Jews, the people the Messiah came to save, and this then properly identifies who is the "we" in Isaiah 53:9. So it would therefore be talking about the work on the cross, not exclusively His earthly ministry.

A possible problem this creates is that now in light of the above, if this applies to the cross, then how could Matthew quote it about Jesus' earthly ministry if Jesus hadn't been to the cross yet up to that point, if this passage in Isaiah is talking about his death?

Something to consider: When Jesus has come down from heaven, and identifies with man, what does He do? He sees oppression, He "frees" the captives; He sees sick people, He heals them; He sees people demon-possessed, He sets people free from demonic captivity. He entered the sufferings of the people. He made people whole, and forgave them.

And He became a sin offering for us. Matthew was writing in retrospect significant time after Jesus' death.

LIE #2: "I'M NOT GOOD ENOUGH"

FORGIVENESS OF SINS IS HEALTHY FOR YOUR BODY

Blessed is the one whose transgression is forgiven, whose sin is covered. Blessed is the man against whom the LORD counts no iniquity, and in whose spirit there is no deceit. For when I kept silent, my bones wasted away through my groaning all day long.

For day and night Your hand was heavy upon me; my strength was dried up as by the heat of summer. Selah. I acknowledged my sin to You, and I did not cover my iniquity; I said, "I will confess my transgressions to the LORD," and You forgave the iniquity of my sin. (Psalm 32:1-5)

NOTICE DAVID in this passage is stating how good it is to be forgiven of sin. Why? Because in his condition, he is arguably under conditions of weakness. He goes to God for forgiveness of his sin which removes those conditions of weakness. Even if the wording here is used figuratively and with no tangible physical weakness present, it's worth noting the language David speaks in. He knew God's goodness would lead him to being restored in his physical condition.

I've heard countless anecdotes of people suffering physical conditions as the result of holding on to bitterness and unforgiveness. I read a secular study once showing the difference between cancer patients with religion and those without, and how a large percentage of the ones "with religion" in the study had lower blood pressure, less stress, and things like that. Even in the natural, unbelieving world there's an understanding that the peace that comes from knowing God brings healing in some fashion to your physical body.

"Man is also rebuked with pain on his bed and with continual strife in his bones, so that his life loathes bread, and his appetite the choicest food.

His flesh is so wasted away that it cannot be seen, and his bones that were not seen stick out. His soul draws near the pit, and his life to those who bring death. If there be for him an angel, a mediator, one of the thousand, to declare to man what is right for him, and he is merciful to him, and says, 'Deliver him from going down into the pit; I have found a ransom; let his flesh become fresh with youth; let him return to the days of his youthful vigor'; then man prays to God, and He accepts him; he sees His face with a shout of joy, and He restores to man his righteousness. He sings before men and says: 'I sinned and perverted what was right, and it was not repaid to me. He has redeemed my soul from going down into the pit, and my life shall look upon the light.' "Behold, God does all these things, twice, three times, with a man, to bring back his soul from the pit, that he may be lighted with the light of life." Job 33:19-30

OK, where do we start?

First of all, notice that in verse 19 it says that this condition of the man being spoken of is a rebuke or, as the King James says, a chastening. This is to serve correction. So let's for one moment entertain the idea of God putting a disease or a sickness on a person — which I believe is the case way less often than most teach and believe. I will not tell someone if they are sick, have a disease, or are ill that they have some sin in their life that has caused God to send judgment on them, but I'm hard pressed to ignore passages like this. Compare this with the account of the Lord causing leprosy to break out on King Uzziah when he tried to offer up unauthorized incense in the temple. He lived a leper the rest of his life as a result of his pride (2 Chronicles 26:16-22).

The conditions Elihu goes on to list here in our passage from Job are undoubtedly describing an actual physical experience, possibly a deathbed experience, since it talks of this person's soul going down to the pit or grave. Verse 23 talks of an angel or mediator of some kind who has found a ransom. Scholars are split on just what or whom the ransom spoken of here is, but read this quote from Matthew Henry's commentary:

> "Jesus Christ is that ransom, so Elihu calls him, as Job had called Him his Redeemer, for He is both the purchaser and the price, the priest and the sacrifice; so high was the value put upon souls that nothing less would redeem them, and so great the injury done by sin that nothing less would atone for it than the blood of the Son of God, who gave his life a ransom for many. This is a ransom of God's finding, a contrivance of Infinite Wisdom; we could never have found it ourselves, and the angels themselves could never have found it."

Matthew 20:28 and 1 Timothy 2:6 indicate Jesus is the ransom for our souls. Even if it can't be concluded accurately that this was foreshadowing Jesus Christ's atonement for the sinner, this is still worth taking into consideration. The way the Hebrew word for ransom, *kopher*, is used elsewhere in Scripture strongly suggests this is an appropriate assumption, but I digress.

Let's change gears slightly. Take a look at the healing miracles Jesus performed in the Gospels. We've already covered earlier why in Scripture healing is provided for in the atonement so I will not belabor that point here. Notice what Jesus says in Luke 13:16, when the Pharisees are on Jesus' case: His response to their accusations that He is breaking the Sabbath is "ought not this woman, a daughter of Abraham whom Satan bound for eighteen years, be loosed from this bond on the Sabbath day?" I don't want to only draw attention to the fact Jesus is basically, on the one hand, saying "the Sabbath day is the *most appropriate* day to heal someone", but the fact He's saying because she's a daughter of Abraham, she should be loosed from the bondage of Satan in her body. The story of Zacchaeus in Luke 19:1-10 bears striking similarities to this story.

We, believers of Jesus Christ, are not sons or daughters of Abraham. Well, we are, but I mean we are saved through the blood of Jesus, and are not under the old covenant like this woman but we have a better one (Hebrews 7:22, 8:6, 12:24). If Jesus made the point that this woman should be healed just because she was a daughter of Abraham, then how much more should we be healed being sons and daughters of the most high God. If the old covenant had promises of healing, then how much more the new one we partake of?

> *And He came down with them and stood on a level place, with a great crowd of His disciples and a great multitude of people from all Judea and Jerusalem and the seacoast of Tyre and Sidon, who came to hear Him and to be healed of their diseases. And those who were troubled with unclean spirits were cured. And all the crowd sought to touch Him, for power came out from Him and healed them all.* (Luke 6:17-19)

Everybody mentioned here in this passage was healed. In a crowd of this magnitude it's more than certain there would be people of all stages of life represented, yet everybody got the exact same result: healing in their body. There'd be people struggling to pay their bills on time and letting that consume their thoughts. There'd be other people struggling with sins in their lives who believed this might be an impediment for Jesus to heal them. Whatever mental roadblock you could think, it's safe to assume people in this crowd probably had struggles just like it.

"BUT YOU DON'T KNOW WHAT I DID!"

One night I went with a native Peruvian worship leader and pastor friend of mine named Dennis Arevelo to an area called Huachipa, outside of Lima, Peru. Since I was still at the stage where I could speak Spanish but still needed an interpreter if I wanted my preaching to hit the mark, we tag teamed a little bit that night. Dennis shared first something on the heart of God, and then afterward I came and shared something a little along the lines of Jesus' eyes of fire watching us.

I thought the direction we were going in was on the love of God and encouraging in that regard, but it was obvious that it was time to do an altar call and invite people forward to repent of anything in their life God needed to purify them of. After a little hesitation, one man came forward, and then another 8 or 9. We prayed with them, and let them spend time alone before God dealing with whatever they needed to deal with before him. But what I want to share is something that happened afterward. It's something I see happen all too often when believers are seeking healing.

Dennis invited people forward if they needed healing in their body, and a few came. I approached the man closest to me and asked him what he needed prayer for, and he told me he had tremendous pain in his back. I encouraged him to stand there and let me pray for him, but immediately I was distracted by his strong crying and sobbing and begging God to forgive him. I tried to encourage him to stop begging God to forgive him, not only for the reason that we don't need to beg God to forgive us — He freely will if we seek after Him to! But because it was hindering his ability to just receive the healing he needed.

I tried encouraging him with this truth, but he proceeded to start telling me what he did. I didn't understand it all because of how slurred and fast the Spanish was. Basically, if I have seen what happened that night once, I've seen it hundreds of times: people believing they've done something or many things so bad they needed some kind of extra special repentance session before God will forgive them.

One of the passages in Scripture I get this confidence from is the prayer of faith found in the epistle of James:

> Is anyone among you sick? Let him call for the elders of the church, and let them pray over him, anointing him with oil in the name of the Lord. And the prayer of faith will save the one who is sick, and the Lord will raise him up. And if he has committed sins, he will be forgiven. (chapter 5:14-15)

Did you notice that? In receiving prayer for the healing of your body, IF you have committed sins, they will be forgiven. Why? Because Jesus' work on the cross was a salvation (deliverance) from both the curse of sin on the body and on the soul. This passage annoys our sensibilities, especially if we've done something so drastic that we have a hard time forgiving ourselves for it; it's all the more difficult to accept that God will forgive us.

Think of someone who has a sexually transmitted disease that they received from a promiscuous lifestyle. They get saved and come to know the Lord, and someone prays for them to be healed, and they DO get healed. I had a roommate in Bible college who had such a thing happen to him. Do you not think then, that if God healed their body, it's a good indication that He always washes over their sin with the same blood that was spilled at Calvary?

Remember the paralytic that was lowered through the roof:

> And when Jesus saw their faith, he said to the paralytic, "Son, your sins are forgiven." Now some of the scribes were sitting there, questioning in their hearts, "Why does this man speak like that? He is blaspheming! Who can forgive sins but God alone?" And immediately Jesus, perceiving in His spirit that they thus questioned within themselves, said to them, "Why do you question these things in your hearts? Which is easier, to say to the paralytic, 'Your sins are forgiven,' or to say, 'Rise, take up your bed and walk'? But that you may know that the Son of Man has authority on earth to forgive sins" — he said to the paralytic — "I say to you, rise, pick up your bed, and go home." (Mark 2:5-11)

Dear saint, the forgiveness of sins is closely intertwined with the healing of the body. In fact, healing your physical body is the much easier of the two, so how much more so can we have confidence that when we go to go God with our conscience weighing us down, not only is He faithful and just to forgive us our sins, but we can be healed in our physical body as well? The problem is too many of us think it should be the other way around, and that we need to be forgiven first before we can get healed, but here are Scriptures that show the two reversed.

Take heart and be encouraged! And by the way, when I prayed for my Peruvian brother that night, in the end he was smiling and rejoicing like he had an "aha" moment, and claimed in the end that his back pain was all gone.

God is good!

LIE #3: "GOD IS WORKING ON MY CHARACTER / GOD IS TEACHING ME A LESSON"

And He went throughout all Galilee, teaching in their synagogues and proclaiming the gospel of the kingdom and healing every disease and every affliction among the people. So His fame spread throughout all Syria, and **they brought Him all the sick***, those afflicted with various diseases and pains, those oppressed by demons, epileptics, and paralytics,* **and He healed them***. And great crowds followed Him from Galilee and the*

Decapolis, and from Jerusalem and Judea, and from beyond the Jordan. (Matthew 4:23-25, emphasis mine)

THIS PASSAGE very closely mirrors the one selected to refute Lie Number One above. In contradiction to the lie that God uses sickness and disease to refine our character — it should be noted that in this crowd — a crowd mind you where *everyone* was healed — there were **demon-possessed** people. These same people who probably had room for improvement as far as their character goes! These individuals did not get healed only after their character was healed, but immediately.

*And Jesus went throughout all the cities and villages, teaching in their synagogues and proclaiming the gospel of the kingdom and healing **every** disease and **every** affliction.* (Matthew 9:35, emphasis mine)

Since everybody was getting healed in these cities and villages — it's highly likely that people of all stages and walks of life would have been represented. Some of them could very well have been taught lessons or been having character refinement in their lives. It didn't matter. Scripturally, we know that if God was refining anybody's character, this would exclude sickness and illness being some kind of method He was using. If God was teaching people lessons using sickness, then Jesus was contradicting or even rebelling against God's plans for these people by healing them. But we know Jesus did what He saw the Father doing.

I'm aware that I'm making a generality in saying the following, and it's not true of everybody, but common enough to state that I've seen many people point to Paul's thorn in the flesh as some kind of proof text regarding this lie.

PAUL'S THORN IN THE FLESH: MESSENGER OF SATAN OR GOD?

I have never watched people live in defeat from misunderstanding a passage as much as this particular misinterpreted passage of Scripture. Of course I'm talking about how people try telling themselves that God gave them a thorn just like Paul's, which I politely hope to show is terrible misinterpretation of Scripture.

It is not disputed that Paul may have had an eye problem in his older age. Numerous scholars and theologians teach this, and research can be found easily on the internet I would imagine. However, it would be bad exegesis to use the passage where Paul talks of a thorn in his flesh to arrive at that conclusion. This passage teaches nothing of the sort, and I hope to unravel a few common traditional thoughts that are tied to it.

In general, our study for the next part of this book will follow like such:

1. What the thorn was
2. What God's reaction was when Paul sought to have it removed
3. Why this subject even matters at all.

I basically will break it down and ask questions, sometimes rhetorical, based on observations on the text. In a way, I've been leading up to this part in particular as one of the most insidious of the lies Christians believe about divine healing. It seemed natural and obvious to include Paul's thorn in this particular lie.

The text I'm referring to is 2 Corinthians 12:7-10:

So to keep me from becoming conceited because of the surpassing greatness of the revelations, a thorn was given me in the flesh, a messenger of Satan to harass me, to keep me from becoming conceited. Three times I pleaded with the Lord about this, that it should leave me. But He said to me, "My grace is sufficient for you, for my power is made perfect in weakness." Therefore I will boast all the more gladly of my weaknesses, so that the power of Christ may rest upon me. For the sake of Christ, then, I am content with weaknesses, insults, hardships, persecutions, and calamities. For when I am weak, then I am strong.

WORD STUDY

FIRST WORD:

Thorn

Strong's number 4647 "*skolops*", meaning "withered at the front, that is, a point or prickle (figuratively a bodily annoyance or disability): — thorn."

Something figurative cannot necessarily be treated as literal in the Word of God. For example, texts in the Psalms refer to God being a strong tower (Psa 61:3), we're also encouraged to take shelter in the shadow of His wings (Psa 91:1), and Jesus said "I am the Bread of Life" (John 6:35). All of this would not literally mean God is a concrete loaf of bread that has wings! But this use of the word *skolops* means it can be referred to as a bodily annoyance.

Other instances of it being used in Scripture can give an idea of what is likely to be meant.

Joshua 23:12-13:

> "*But if you turn away and ally yourselves with the survivors of these nations that remain among you and if you intermarry with them and associate with them, then you may be sure that the LORD your God will no longer drive out these nations before you. Instead, they will become snares and traps for you, whips on your backs and*

thorns in your eyes, until you perish from this good land, which the LORD your God has given you."

In this context, the "thorn" has a negative connotation, and is a source of pain and annoyance as a result of failing to drive out the nations in the land Israel is possessing. Thorns are a result of disobedience. Here, God allowed them but was not the author or originator of the whips on their back or thorns in their eyes. It was their disobedience and this would be a reminder to them perpetually in generations to come.

Ezekiel 28:24:

> "No longer will the people of Israel have malicious neighbors who are painful briers and sharp thorns. Then they will know that I am the Sovereign LORD."

Again, notice that the Lord promises at one point to remove this thorn. In both texts used so far, thorns are referred to as people — both in the sense that they are "enemies" of God's people. For other examples, please look at Isaiah 55:13, Hosea 10:8 and Micah 7:4.

Our next word to look at will demonstrate why I personally don't accept that God was the one who gave Paul the thorn. I've had someone tell me recently "if God or Paul wanted us to know what the thorn was, we would have been told so". Well, if we read the text we can find out it was a "messenger of Satan'.

Second word:

Messenger [of Satan]

Strong's number 32, *aggelos*: "a messenger; especially an *angel*; by implication a pastor: angel, messenger."

First, observe the messenger is clearly stated as being from SATAN. That's reason enough to conclude that God didn't put this thorn in Paul's side!

Second, the messenger is a person or an angel, and clearly NOT a disease.

This Greek word *aggelos* appears 188 times in the Bible and is translated *angel* 181 times, and *messenger* the other 7 times. In all 188 instances, it is without exception, a person and not a thing.

Examples of this word being used in Scripture — and translated differently — will demonstrate what Paul is saying and referring to. The times that the word *aggelos* is translated as messenger are verses such as Matt 10:11, Mark 1:2 and Luke 7:27 which invariably say

> *"Behold, I send my messenger (aggelos) before your face, who will prepare your way before you."*

Notice how it's translated in Matthew 25:31:

> *"When the Son of Man comes in His glory, and all the*

angels (aggelos) with Him, then He will sit on His glorious throne."

Consider that the thorn was not a physical disease, but a *personal figure*. The same with a messenger of Satan. It's now twice as easy to understand what Paul was dealing with since we are told two things, not just one. The second qualifies the first.

We learn from this word study that the literal definition is either an angel or it's implied in the Greek that it could mean a pastor. From reading the context we see Paul is in no way talking about a physical problem, but after reading chapter 1 1, we're more inclined to see how he could likely be referring to persecution.

ALTERNATIVE EXPLANATION

"For if someone comes to you and preaches a Jesus other than the Jesus we preached, or if you receive a different spirit from the one you received, or a different gospel from the one you accepted, you put up with it easily enough. But I do not think I am in the least inferior to those "superapostles".

And I will keep on doing what I am doing in order to cut the ground from under those who want an opportunity to be considered equal with us in the things they boast about. For such men are false apostles, deceitful workmen, masquerading as apostles of Christ. And no wonder, for Satan himself masquerades as an angel of light. It is not surprising, then, if his servants masquerade as servants of righteousness. Their end will be what their actions deserve." (2 Cor 11:4-5, 12-15)

For almost all of the rest of chapter 11 Paul lists all sorts of things he's been through as an apostle, such as shipwrecks and imprisonments. Of all the things Paul mentions, not one of them is a sickness or perpetual infirmity! Sickness and disease are conspicuous by their absence — especially in light of the fact that most interpret Paul's thorn as a sickness. However, the physical things he mentions in this list are things like beatings, floggings, and fastings, but not one mention of sickness.

So with that flow of thought in mind, and after pouring his heart of love out in writing to the Corinthians about his concern, would Paul really suddenly refer to a disease or sickness in an abstract way that has nothing to do with what he's been talking about? It's highly improbable.

Paul's thorn is popularly taught to be an eye problem, ophthalmia. I don't dispute whether he had such a problem because there's credible evidence elsewhere in Scripture that he *might* have, but I believe this text isn't one that supports it. I submit to you for consideration, based on the evidence I've provided so far, that the thorn was in fact more likely to be a person — maybe a false apostle, or an angelic figure (demon). Judging from reading statements he peppers 1 and 2 Corinthians with — this person or these people were false messengers of the Gospel who likely were hindering Paul's Gospel work and scattering his flock.

Also, does God give revelation to us and then change His mind and beat us half to death because He gave us too much? If the revelation of the things of God were what caused God to give him the thorn, to keep him from becoming too conceited, why would God have given him or allowed Paul to obtain such "greatness of revelation" in the first place? Why would God then turn around and say "Oops, I accidentally gave you too much knowledge and revelation — have this thorn in your side"? There are lots of things God can use to keep people from being too highly exalted, but the following texts show it was not God who orchestrated this in Paul's life or in his physical body.

MY GRACE IS SUFFICIENT?

We are so sickness-minded in the Body of Christ that we just think God wants us to tolerate everything the devil throws at us and go to the doctor instead of appropriating what The Doctor already gave us.

> But He said to me, "My grace is sufficient for you, for My power is made perfect in weakness." Therefore I will boast all the more gladly of my weaknesses, so that the

*power of Christ may rest upon me. For the sake of Christ,
then, I am content with weaknesses, insults, hardships,
persecutions, and calamities. For when I am weak, then I
am strong.* (2 Corinthians 12:9-10)

Nowhere does this Scripture insinuate — even if you keep
reading — that God was unwilling to do anything about
the thorn in Paul's flesh. In fact, I would like to take you
on a quick journey of why I feel God already answered
Paul's problem before he went to the Lord, and just
wanted to remind him of it.

WORD STUDY

First word:

Grace

GK 5485 *charis.* From G5463 "graciousness (as gratify-
ing), of manner or act (abstract or concrete; literal, figurative or spiritual; especially the divine influence upon the
heart, and its reflection in the life; including gratitude):
acceptable, benefit, favour, gift, grace (-ious), joy liberality,
pleasure, thank (-s, -worthy)."

This word never gets translated into words like *mercy* or
compassion from Greek to English, and those two words
come from different roots. When studying a word and its
context in Scripture it's necessary — if we really want to
grasp its meaning — to go to the original source and

compare other instances of it being translated; whether as another word, or just how it's used in other contexts. An English definition for a word will not give as clear of an idea of what the author of Scripture is saying as does the original language (in this New Testament instance, Greek).

Of the 155 times *charis* is translated grace, only half or so actually mean something like *unmerited favor*. For examples of it denoting a divine ability, enabling, or gifting the reader is invited to check out Luke 2:40, Acts 4:33 and 6:8, and Romans 1:5, 12:3 and 12:6. It's clear from the immediate context of these verses that although grace is unmerited favor, there's another layer to it denoting spiritual power or ability in these passages.

Another instance of this word *charis* being used:

> *Therefore, since we have been justified by faith, we have peace with God through our Lord Jesus Christ. Through Him we have also obtained access by faith into this grace (charis) in which we stand, and we rejoice in hope of the glory of God. More than that, we rejoice in our sufferings, knowing that suffering produces endurance, and endurance produces character, and character produces hope, and hope does not put us to shame, because God's love has been poured into our hearts through the Holy Spirit who has been given to us.* (Romans 5:1-5)

An Old Testament example of God speaking to a man in a

similar way as He did to Paul here is found in the life of Moses, in Exodus. When Moses brought Israel to the sea he cried out to God, who responded in a way that would offend most Christians:

> "Why do you cry to Me? Tell the people of Israel to go forward. Lift up your staff, and stretch out your hand over the sea and divide it, that the people of Israel may go through the sea on dry ground." (Exodus 14:15-16).

I can almost picture the Lord saying it like "Why are you bothering to come to me about it? I already gave you what you need — now use it — lift up your rod!" Likewise, Paul is being told "What I've already given you (grace/charis/enablement) is all you need."

Second word:

Power

GK 1411 *dunamis* From G1410; "force (literally or figuratively); specifically miraculous power (usually by implication a miracle itself): ability, abundance, meaning, might (-ily, -y, -y deed), (worker of) miracle (-s), power, strength, violence, mighty (wonderful) work."

The following verses, showing power/*dunamis* being used elsewhere, should show that Paul is not being told that God has just enough power for Paul's emotions to be settled while he goes through whatever horrible thing he goes through. Rather, power is usually used in Scripture for miraculous denotation:

> *And when Peter saw it he addressed the people: "Men of Israel, why do you wonder at this, or why do you stare at us, as though by our own **power** or piety we have made him walk?"* Acts 3:12

> *And when they had set them in the midst, they inquired, "By what **power** or by what name did you do this?"* Acts 4:7

> *And with great **power** the apostles were giving their testimony to the resurrection of the Lord Jesus, and great **grace** [charis, again used here] was upon them all.* Acts 4:33

> *On one of those days, as He was teaching, Pharisees and teachers of the law were sitting there, who had come from every village of Galilee and Judea and from Jerusalem. And the **power** of the Lord was with him to heal.* Luke 5:17

> *Behold, I have given you authority to tread on serpents and scorpions, and over all the **power** of the enemy, and nothing shall hurt you.* Luke 10:19 — though this is in a negative context, it still serves the purpose of demonstrating the word's use.

> *And behold, I am sending the promise of my Father upon*

you. But stay in the city until you are clothed with **power** *from on high.* Luke 24:49

THIRD WORD:

Weakness

GK 769 *astheneia*

"From G772; feebleness (of body or mind); by implication malady; moral frailty: — disease, infirmity, sickness, weakness."

Yes, this word does mean weakness or malady. I almost didn't even really need to show that to you to prove my point. However, depending on the translation of the Scriptures you read, Paul lists 5 or 6 things, of which this word *astheneia* is one. That means there's a 1 in 6 chance — or 5 if you want to go by whatever English translation you use that only has 5 listed and not 6 — that at the forefront of Paul's mind he's likely referring to his thorn as being a malady.

> *So for the sake of Christ, I am well pleased and take pleasure in infirmities, insults, hardships, persecutions, perplexities and distresses* (v.10, Amplified Bible)

NON-TRADITIONAL APPROACH

Contrary to what is popularly taught, and based on what

the text says, I hope this clears up some confusion people may have concerning:

1. What Paul's thorn was,
2. That God did *not* give it to Him; and
3. That God's reaction to Paul is not what is usually taught — that He just kind of told Paul to tolerate it.

I hope you can see why we've spent considerably more time on this particular lie than the other ones combined.

From what we've already established as being the context of the previous chapter in Paul's letter, it's very clear sickness is not on Paul's mind, but he's saying in passing that it's one of the things he doesn't let get him down and lets Christ be magnified through. If we consider his ministry to the Gentiles, and look at things Paul wrote elsewhere, and from just plain reading the book of Acts, we can safely assume that Paul would have walked in relatively divine health if he was healing people and ministering with signs and wonders following. Therefore, it's feasible that something *else* (or some*one* else) is the thorn he has just referred to.

WHY DOES IT MATTER?

As mentioned, it is commonly taught without much dispute that Paul had an eye disease based on a few circumstantial Scripture references revolving around 2 Corinthians 12:7-10 as our anchor, and that he could barely see as a result. In fact, the conditions of this disease are such that he would have had pus oozing out of his eyes down his face at any given moment. I hope to show just a few reasons why this view is really preposterous.

Acts 19:11-12 says

> "And God was doing extraordinary miracles by the hands of Paul, so that even handkerchiefs or aprons that had touched his skin were carried away to the sick, and their diseases left them and the evil spirits came out of them."

Now correct me if I'm wrong, but if someone had such a contagious and disgusting eye disease would we really be passing around handkerchiefs they used in order to heal sick people, and cast out demons with them? Or would we not burn them or dispose of them in order to avoid having the infection spread? Of course not; we'd do all we could to avoid having others get contaminated!

If the Bible is clear about something there is no discussion needed on it. If the Bible is ambiguous about something then people are free to have their own opinions on it. However, the Bible is not vague on this topic or this passage, but very clear. It's our *perception* of these passages and our "faith eyeglasses" that need fixing. If we let the Scripture merely say what it says, we'd have way less confusion in the Body of Christ, and certainly way fewer people living in defeat when it comes to seeing a healing in their life. A false understanding of this passage, and ones seemingly like it, has held untold multitudes of believers back from receiving healing in their physical bodies.

I have yet to find someone in opposition to the subject of divine healing who does NOT bring up the issue of Paul's thorn, believing it to be some kind of "aha" Scripture that demolishes any further discussion on the matter. As such, any further discussion or study on the subject should at least deal with this particular roadblock for many hungry seekers of the truth.

WHO REALLY CARES WHAT THE THORN WAS OR WHO IT CAME FROM?

I remember when I once had a discussion with someone whom I've known for a long time. She had a condition that she attributed to her sinful past, and upon trying to encourage her, using the Word of God to show that He wants (i.e. *wills*) to take this away from her, she insisted she was being taught a lesson by the Lord about sowing and reaping. She told me that she's destined to bear this burden. Wouldn't you guess it, her Scriptural support in her mind was that "even Paul had a thorn".

I've thought about this numerous times ever since, and in other conversations where people are living in defeat or they're just plain sick from something but don't want to believe they can be made whole or well. If what I've just spent the last little while sharing with you is wrong, then let's hypothetically concede Paul having had a disease or sickness God put on him as a "thorn in his side". We would then also need to take into account the rest of the passage preceding it, which sadly, few Christians can possibly say they live up to: the surpassing greatness of revelations like Paul had. If anybody wanted to be honest with themselves, they'd have to admit they are *not* on the same playing field as Paul in this regard.

We only covered the subject of Paul's thorn in the flesh in a cursory manner in just one chapter. If you'd like to study this a bit more, my friend Art Thomas has gone more in depth with this in his own book, *Spiritual Tweezers: Removing Paul's "Thorn in the Flesh" and Other False Objections to God's Will for Healing.*

LIE #4: "SICKNESS IS HOW WE DIE"

I WISH to be respectful of any who are reading this and may have lost a loved one to cancer or terminal disease. It may be a fact that it has happened, and nothing can be done now, and you may struggle with my saying this, but it was *not* God's best intention for them — especially if they weren't believers! It's the enemy, Satan, who seeks to steal, kill and destroy (John 10:10).

We WILL die one day, the same way a car wears out and eventually a new one is needed. This is inevitable. But that doesn't mean we blow the car up one day and then decide to buy a new one.

I've had people say to me that if God wanted to heal everybody, then nobody would die. This sounds logical, but it's flawed reasoning. I will try answering this question by reframing the premise. If sin brought death, and Jesus' atonement redeemed us from the curse of the fall of Adam which was death and sickness (incipient death), then why do we still die?

These thoughts are controversial, and nobody reading this will agree 100% with me, and I'm not trying to provide pat answers in order to uphold my doctrine. I hate when people do that to me–when people don't want to back down from their views, but ignore pertinent Scriptures or just plain rationalize things away. I once wrote this next portion over 6 years ago for my personal blog, and I've since reworked it over time the more I learned different things.

I realize I'll never completely be able to provide satisfactory answers for everybody, but give the following some thought for encouragement.

THE LAST ENEMY IS DEATH

Let's begin by keeping in mind that 1 Corinthians 15:26 states that the *last* enemy to be destroyed is death. It tells us death is still "here" until that happens. The context being that this is taught usually as a rapture passage — I don't think it is, for how can we be changed at the *last* trumpet unless there are other trumpets first? I will not go there at this time, other than pointing out for this subject matter that passage describing the end of history. The passage states:

> *I tell you this, brothers: flesh and blood cannot inherit the kingdom of God, nor does the perishable inherit the imperishable.*
>
> *Behold! I tell you a mystery. We shall not all sleep [die], but we shall all be changed, in a moment, in the twinkling of an eye, at the last trumpet. For the trumpet will sound, and the dead will be raised imperishable, and we shall be changed.*
>
> *For this perishable body must put on the imperishable, and this mortal body must put on immortality.*
>
> *When the perishable puts on the imperishable, and the*

mortal puts on immortality, then shall come to pass the saying that is written: "Death is swallowed up in victory."

"O death, where is your victory? O death, where is your sting?"

The sting of death is sin, and the power of sin is the law.

But thanks be to God, who gives us the victory through our Lord Jesus Christ. (1 Corinthians 15:50-57, parentheses mine)

Verse 50 makes clear that flesh and blood cannot inherit the kingdom of God. Is it not true that for now we are clothed in flesh and blood, *perishable* mortal bodies (v. 53)?

The text also states we're going to have glorified *new bodies* in heaven and not what we've got now. I've had people say to me that since we get new bodies at that time, then there's no point in having our bodies healed now in this lifetime. These can go ahead and practice what they preach if that's what they'd like.

Others say "the ultimate healing is in death". My response to that is to invite these to stay sick with their illness or problem for the rest of their earthly life until they die, if that's what they want to believe. This shocks most people, but it shouldn't if they truthfully believe what they claim. Who on earth and in their right mind will want to keep an illness or an infirmity for the rest of their earthly life if that burden could be removed from them in this lifetime? Remember that Jesus healed physical "perishable bodies" in His earthly lifetime, even though those people would go on to die one day anyway, so just pointing out that Jesus healed people makes the "we're all going to die one day" a moot point. Also keep in mind how Romans 8:11 says,

> *"If the Spirit of Him who raised Jesus from the dead dwells in you, He who raised Christ Jesus from the dead will also give life to your **mortal** bodies through His Spirit who dwells in you."*

Furthermore, keep in mind that in His earthly ministry, Jesus did not raise all the dead. In fact, the accounts of the dead being raised in the Gospels are typically of young people, or those who died suddenly from sicknesses — "before their time" if you will. Those are the types of people He raised from the dead, but then of course they eventually died later anyway.

We're not told how old Lazarus lived to be. We're not told how long Jairus' daughter lived after being raised from the dead, or what age the widow's son lived to be. I believe, they would have lived on to fulfill their purpose and destiny. This is based on Hebrews 9:27 which says *"it is appointed once to die, then after that comes the judgment"*.

If this passage is true — which all Scripture is! — and if

what most teach concerning the Sovereignty of God is true, then Jesus was messing up the Father's plan by raising from the dead those that the Father had appointed to die. In fact, how do we handle the fact there are people in human history and in the Gospel records who died twice—the people Jesus raised from the dead, who died later for good? A kingdom divided against itself cannot stand (Matt 12:25). Jesus never did anything in rebellion or contradiction to the Father, but only did what He saw His Father doing (John 5:19). So if Jesus raised people from the dead, it means the Father wanted Jesus to do so, implying the Father didn't want those peoples' lives ended at that time. Does Father God have multiple personalities? Does He "kill people" and then raise them again? Of course not!

The thing to keep in mind is the word *appointed*. Things happen that aren't God's will many times in Scripture. For example, how can God regret doing anything, if it's not what He originally intended? Our own life experiences demonstrate this also — but God is bigger than the devil and can do a good job at cleaning up the devil's mess. So good, in fact, that we forget there ever was a mess and conclude the thing must have been God's will all along because of what good we saw come out of it. This also in many ways answers the way God can will for everyone to be healed, *but not all get healed*. This also explains how He's not willing that *any* should perish (1 Timothy 2:4, 2 Peter 3:9), but that hell having a population of at least one soul proves something being God's will doesn't guarantee it to come to pass. Diseases, cancer or terminal illnesses are not God's way of "bringing people home". It may have happened to a loved one in your family, and you believe without a shadow of a doubt that it was their time to go, or that God was the Author of it. I will sympathize with your loss, and I will never argue with you about it. But from Scripture it's hard to conclude this is how God does it, and I will not settle for it in my own life.

WHY DO SO MANY CHRISTIANS BELIEVE GOD AND SATAN ARE TEAMMATES?

I don't believe in something called "sickness unto death". It comes side-by-side with something some Christians believe in called the "sickness unto chastisement" teaching. It teaches that God puts certain sicknesses on us that we will die from. The only Scripture I reasonably come up with is 2 Kings 13:14 which states

> "Now when Elisha had fallen sick with the illness of which he was to die..."

It would behoove us to realize the fact that this is one sentence mentioning his illness in passing. It doesn't imply anything. It's just a statement of fact. We are not told what it was, and that there's no real New Testament example of something similar, unless people cling tightly to the idea Paul's thorn in the flesh was a sickness, but we've already disproved that it was a sickness or infirmity.

Why do so many believers think we all have to die of something? Don't many people NOT die of cancer, or heart attacks? Is it that hard to believe our earthly suits will just stop working one day and we'll go home? Don't some die in their sleep peacefully? Don't some just one day drop dead for no reason in particular other than old age, and "give up the ghost"? Why is it so many Christians are pessimistic instead of optimistic when it comes to healing and sicknesses?!

"Sickness unto chastisement" is a lie based on 1 Corinthians 11 when Paul wrote to the church at Corinth who were partaking unworthily of the Lord's Supper. It's worth observing that the sicknesses and people falling ill were **judgment** for the way they partook of this covenant meal! These persons had a lack of "covenant protection" resulting in death.

This doesn't mean that God is smiting them for partaking it in an unworthy manner. Think of it this way: if I am given an umbrella to use in the pouring rain, and I step outside without it, I'll get wet if it's raining. It doesn't mean God "sent the rain" on me to punish me for not using an umbrella. It simply means that, I didn't use the protection of the umbrella and suffered the consequences.

Do *all* who get sick fall ill because they're under judgment from God? Absolutely not! If someone asks me to pray for them, do I tell them the reason they're sick is judgment from God? Heck no! I encourage you to do your job as a Spirit-filled believer in Christ and lay your hands on them and proclaim healing through the blood of Jesus. James 5 states the elders will pray for the sick, they will be healed, and whatever sins they've committed will be forgiven simultaneously as they're being healed of sickness.

The New Testament examples we see, such as this one mentioned, involve God *judging sin*. Obedient children of God following Him have no need of worrying God will judge them if they're obediently following Him. This "sickness unto death"/chastisement stuff from what I can tell, does little other than make people wonder if God is upset with them if they fall ill, instead of looking at their real enemy who may more than likely be the real perpetrator.

It should be noted, unfortunately, in most places I look I notice also in all these articles and books that sickness usually is never viewed as a curse or a *bad* thing by an alarming number of Christians. Nor is the idea that the devil is ever involved usually given any credence. Instead, it's usually the "Lord works in mysterious ways and who are we to question what He allows us to go through". I'll tell you why you should question it — because you could be wrong, and finding out the truth could change your situation around! No wonder many people don't believe it's the Lord's will to heal them if this is the kind of stuff they're being taught! No wonder we don't see more heal-ings and miracles — we get what we teach and preach for!

PHYSICAL DEATH

This may shock you that I'd say, or it might not ring right in your ears, but I believe that death, in that we all die one day — because it's appointed once for all to die — is unre-lated to healing, sickness, restoration and the Atonement. Hear me out before you assume I'm contradicting myself, or sounding like I'm a politician talking out of both sides of my mouth.

Death, in that we live out our lives and then one day "give up the ghost" and go home, is a matter of going home when our numbered days are completed. God doesn't "kill us". Oftentimes in the Scriptures, He seems to bring His children home. On the one hand, Hebrews 9:27 states that we are appointed to die once and then after that face judgment. This is held in tension with other passages that tell us of honoring our parents that we may live long life (Exodus 20:12, Deut 5:16, Ephesians 6:3). There are also references throughout the Psalms and Proverbs that tell us if we hold fast to wisdom, or we obey the Lord He'll lengthen the days of our lives, or we don't have to worry about various pestilences that befall the wicked (see Psalm 91, for example).

The devil on the other hand seeks to steal, kill and destroy, and in other words take from us what God gives and has given us — and bring that last day to pass sooner than appointed. It's true, people do stupid things by way of accident or negligence that God sometimes doesn't intervene and prevent. But keep in mind, it's the devil whose whole mission and modus operandus is to rob us of our earthly callings and he takes people out, and it's not God's will. I will not tackle Calvnistic viewpoints on the sovereignty of God, and I will not cover the subject of martyrdom in this book on purpose because I want to keep this book short.

Persecution, trials and tribulation will be the lot in the believer's life. However, we have no reason to expect physical sickness to be something God is the author of.

In Genesis 3:22-23, when Adam and Eve were punished for their disobedience, God said:

> *Behold, the man has become like one of us in knowing good and evil. Now, lest he reach out his hand and take also of the tree of life and eat, and live forever—" therefore the LORD God sent him out from the garden of Eden to work the ground from which he was taken.*

According to this passage, God kept Adam out of the Garden of Eden after this *so that* he would not reach out and eat from the other tree as well–remember, there were two trees in the Garden (Genesis 2:9). The Lord told Adam that in the day that he ate of the tree of knowledge of good and evil — not to be confused with the tree of life

— he'd surely die. Did either Eve or Adam die on the very day they ate the fruit? No? Then what's to be made of this 'death'? Was it just spiritual death?

Notice that the Lord told Adam not to eat of the tree of the knowledge of good and evil, but in Genesis 3:2-3, Eve tells the serpent its the tree of *life* they're not to eat, or they'll die. Well which was it they were not to eat? Were they not to eat either one? Or was she confused and speaking wrongly, since after all, it wasn't her directly that the Lord gave this instruction to, since she wasn't even created yet when the Lord instructed Adam about this? Was she adding to what she was told?

Consider this: In order for God to banish them so that they won't eat of the tree of life and live forever, it implies they were not going to live forever unless they ate it. This was *after* they sinned and were now in a fallen state. Death and sin entered creation as a result of their disobedience. Before automatically assuming what I've been saying and am about to say is heresy, give it some thought and go over the first three chapters of Genesis carefully — I still am doing so, and have a lot more confidence in what I'm saying here the more I meditate on it. When reading commentaries and doing searches on the internet typing in "if God wills to heal all, then why do all still die", I don't find pages that deal with this passage, so I'm hard pressed to find correct interpretations of this but submit this to you for your consideration. Especially if it will help encourage you and make a fighter out of you where the enemy is concerned!

God's refusing to allow Adam and Eve to eat of the tree of life now that they were corrupt and defiled was an act of his mercy. He didn't want man living forever in their sinful flesh, and in a fallen world. That would be hell. Hell is eternity in sin cut off from the Lord, and if Adam ate of the fruit from the tree of life, it would not have been much better than an eternity in hell will be.

The book of Revelation says we will at that future time get to eat of the tree of life. In the meantime, until our life-span is over, God can and does 'patch up' our bodies to keep working, but we don't get a brand new body in this lifetime.

TO SUMMARIZE

To reiterate, our healing in our current bodies — our redemption and our restoration — has been purchased for us in this lifetime. Are all fully enjoying physical healing 100% of the time? To answer that question let me pose another question: are we enjoying the full benefits — in this lifetime — of anything God's given us? Are we fully enjoying the benefits of having our sins forgiven? Physical death has everything to do to with resurrection. Can you be resurrected if you're not dead?

In closing, Isaiah 33:20-24 describes the new Zion where God's people will dwell:

> Behold Zion, the city of our appointed feasts! Your eyes will see Jerusalem, an untroubled habitation, an immovable tent, whose stakes will never be plucked up, nor will any of its cords be broken.
>
> But there the LORD in majesty will be for us a place of broad rivers and streams, where no galley with oars can go, nor majestic ship can pass.
>
> For the LORD is our judge; the LORD is our lawgiver; the LORD is our king; He will save us.
>
> Your cords hang loose; they cannot hold the mast firm in its place or keep the sail spread out. Then prey and spoil in abundance will be divided; even the lame will take the prey.
>
> And no inhabitant will say, "I am sick"; the people who dwell there will be forgiven their iniquity.

Notice verse 24 brings up how nobody will be sick because their sins are forgiven. The two are related — and in this time spoken of here, the full revelation and embodiment of what has been purchased on the cross in the atonement of Christ will be realized.

You can wait until then to see healing in your body if you want to. But I'm still going for it in *this* lifetime, based on what the Word of God says.

"Your kingdom come, your will be done, on earth as it is in heaven." (Matthew 6:10)

It is true that some do, and have died from sicknesses and diseases, but that doesn't mean it was God's will or how He wanted to take them home. The enemy comes specifically to steal and kill and destroy but Christ has have come that we may have life, and have it to the full (John 10:10).

LIE #5: "I DON'T HAVE ENOUGH FAITH"

USUALLY THE PERSON saying this is referring to themselves, yet Jesus healed people whether they had faith to be healed or not. The only people throughout the New Testament Jesus ever told they didn't have enough faith was His disciples — the healers.

WHOSE FAITH IS IT, ANYWAY?

A common reason I've heard sincere and well-meaning believers use that justifies their not believing for miracles or divine healing is the idea that "God wills some to be sick" or there's some "divine purpose" behind someone's disease or infirmity.

"I prayed, and the sickness never went away, so I guess it's God's will for me to be sick."

The texts for our consideration are found in Matthew 17:14-21, Mark 9:14-29, Luke 9:37-43a. Each account details the time when a man brought his epileptic boy to the disciples and they were unable to heal him.

To glean from and paraphrase all three accounts, the situation goes something like this: Jesus came down from the mountain after His transfiguration. Mark records that the disciples were in a relatively heated argument — or as the Greek here literally means, a "joint investigation". In other words, the scribes and the disciples were trying to figure out how come the disciples were unable to cast the demon out of this man's son.

It should be noted before going any further that in Matthew 10 and Luke 9:1-6, Jesus had already sent out the disciples in His name to preach and heal and cast out demons — and demonstrate the kingdom of the One who sent them in His name. So, the disciples have already been endued with authority to do such things, such as the case here with his man's son. However, now they are unable to for some reason. At this point chronologically in each Gospel account this is recorded in, they've already done such deliverances and performed healings themselves, through the power of God in them. They are experienced on some level and have seen results already, so the question that comes up is: Why no result *this* time? What's different?

Two spiritual matters are brought to light in this story, and usually only one of the two is focused on: this passage is usually shown to teach how certain demons can only be cast out of people by prayer and fasting. I will challenge that assumption in a moment. We tend to forget what Jesus told this man, and what He told his disciples privately later:

> *"But if you can do anything, have compassion on us and help us." And Jesus said to him, "If you can! All things are possible for one who believes." Immediately the father of the child cried out and said, "I believe; help my unbelief!"* (Mark 9:22-24)

UNBELIEF AND LACK OF FAITH ARE A KEY COMPONENT OF THE ISSUE

I've always wondered if Jesus was being slightly sarcastic when he said "If you can!" in response to this man's plea. If this man knew more about Jesus before bringing his son to the disciples, he probably would've known Jesus *can*, but probably the lack of ability on the part of Jesus' disciples made him second-guess if Jesus *could*. As Matthew Henry states in his commentary on this passage *"Thus Christ suffers in his honour by the difficulties and follies of his disciples."* And so it still is to this day.

Jesus rebuked the demon, and it came out of the boy. Everyone glorified God, and Jesus entered the house He was on his way to, and the disciples then came up to Him and asked Him why they were unable to cast it out. You have more than likely heard and remembered that He tells them *"this kind can only go out by prayer and fasting".* However, if you've got a good Bible, there will be a note there at the end of Mark 9:29, and some translations of your Bibles will not even have verse 21 in Matthew 17, which also states the same thing.

Matthew's Gospel records another component as to why they were unable to cast out the demon:

> *Because of your little faith. For truly, I say to you, if you have faith like a grain of mustard seed, you will say to this mountain, "Move from here to there," and it will move, and nothing will be impossible for you.* (Matthew 17:20)

Because of a lack of faith.

WHY DOES ANY OF THIS EVEN MATTER?

If you ever want to make someone feel insulted, just imply that they lack faith for something. Even if you don't say it, people somehow pick up on it and assume that if you're saying people can have more faith for things, that it necessitates people already don't have enough faith.

Well, that's exactly what I'm saying. Try not to be offended about it if you feel I'm talking about you, because I am. This applies to all of us for at least two reasons.

1. Faith is measurable
2. This passage also shows that just because healing didn't happen (initially anyway) doesn't mean it was God's will for someone to stay sick

All believers have a "seed" — if you will — of faith, but each of us waters it and feeds it at our own pace, our own amount, on our own frequency. Some people move mighty mountains, while others buckle under pressure if they don't know how they'll pay their $30 credit card bill that month. Frankly, NOT everybody has the same amount of faith — and I don't care if it's politically incorrect or rude to say so, either.

However, I personally will **never** step on somebody for not believing as hard for something as I do, any more than I'd kick a baby for not walking yet. The Bible says of Jesus *"a bruised reed he will not break, and a smoldering wick he will not quench"* (Matt. 12:20). We need to be patient as believers with each other and not get frustrated with someone just because they aren't where we are yet. Build them up. Edify them *into* what you're showing them, don't just prove them wrong and think that settles it. We should show others ways to increase their faith, but not jump on them for not being there yet and put blame and guilt on them.

Maybe it's possible, after all the things the disciples had already done in their ministry with Jesus, they had not yet seen something this severe and were not ready to handle it? Is it possible maybe that they weren't mature enough in their faith yet to handle this particular deliverance properly? Who knows, I'm just speculating and any other assumption from the text is just that — speculation. But Jesus did tell them they had "little faith", and we can't ignore that, even if it's not seeker sensitive or politically correct.

If I were to say to someone–no, if I were to insinuate or simply IMPLY they were unable to obtain results in something because of little faith, I'd never hear the end of it from people about how arrogant I am.

But this is an honest explanation Jesus, God Himself, gave His own disciples. It's worth considering carefully and learning from.

DOES FAITH THE SIZE OF A MUSTARD SEED REALLY MOVE MOUNTAINS?

That passage is obviously *not* what this passage is teaching. Jesus can't be talking here of the size of a mustard seed if he just told his disciples the reason they couldn't do something was because the size of "their faith seed" was too small. We learn from other passages where the kingdom of God is described as a mustard seed, that it starts off small, but then grows and dominates the garden (Luke 13: 18-19). Maybe our "faith" is something that grows and increases in time if it possesses the very characteristics of the example used to describe it — a mustard seed.

Let's detour for a moment and focus on that before going further in our text at hand.

Have you ever heard that statement "all you need is faith the size of a mustard seed and you can move a mountain"? The idea behind it, whenever most Christians quote it, is that you don't need very much faith to do something huge. It actually comes from a misunderstanding of the Word that faith is not measurable, but we all have the same proportion. The body of Christ needs to do away with this cliché that misinterprets Scripture.

Let's look at one of the instances in the Gospel where Jesus says this. This teaching leads people to teach and encourage other believers to think this passage says they don't have to do anything. Faith "the size of a mustard seed" is used to justify doing little to nothing, rather than provoking tenacity of faith to see the things of God.

And when they came to the crowd, a man came up to him

*and, kneeling before him, said, "Lord, have mercy on my son, for he is an epileptic and he suffers terribly. For often he falls into the fire, and often into the water. And I brought him to your disciples, **and they could not heal him.**" And Jesus answered, "O faithless and twisted generation, how long am I to be with you? How long am I to bear with you? Bring him here to me." And Jesus rebuked him, and the demon came out of him, and the boy was healed instantly. Then the disciples came to Jesus privately and said, "Why could we not cast it out?" He said to them, "Because of your little faith. For truly, I say to you, if you have faith like a grain of mustard seed, you will say to this mountain, "Move from here to there," and it will move, and nothing will be impossible for you."* (Matthew 17:14-20, emphasis mine)

Notice how in this particular passage, Jesus tells them it's *because* of their little faith that they were unable to heal the boy. This translation accurately avoids translating it "faith as small" as a mustard seed. Context shows it cannot be talking about the *size* of your faith, since Jesus just rebuked his disciples for not having big enough faith! Jesus didn't suffer from multiple personality disorder!

So where do we come up with this misinterpretation, and how did it become such a cliché we use often in Christian circles? I really don't know. But now let me ask you something: if all it took was a tiny mustard seed to move mountains, then how come there is still quite a lot the Church is currently unable to see take place in the way of miracles and logic-defying deeds? If all it took was a mustard seed, then I'd hate to be the devil when a Christian has more than a mustard seed of faith!

There are five incidents in the New Testament where the mustard seed is referred to, each found in the Gospels. Luke 17:6 is almost identical to this passage, but is in a different context from the above quoted Scripture. The other three come up in a different parable — the parable about the kingdom of heaven. Matt 13:31 is almost identical to its counterparts in the other gospels:

> "It is **like** a grain of mustard seed, which, when sown on the ground, is the smallest of all the seeds on earth, yet when it is sown it grows up and **becomes larger** than all the garden plants and puts out large branches, so that the birds of the air can make nests in its shade." (Mark 4:31-32, emphasis mine)

> He said therefore, "What is the kingdom of God like? And to what shall I compare it? It is **like** a grain of mustard seed that a man took and sowed in his garden, and i**t grew** and became a tree, and the birds of the air made nests in its branches." (Luke 13:18-19, emphasis mine)

This passage gets confused in peoples' minds with the teaching of Jesus concerning speaking to the mountain, and therefore the teachings get mixed together and we've come up with this idea it's OK to have little faith. In context that's clearly *not* what Jesus taught his disciples.

Could it be, based on this explanation as to what a mustard seed is and what it does, that we can glean from this parable — which uses the same illustration — and learn something that can change our understanding of the other passage?

Our faith is to be like a mustard seed. What is a mustard seed like? Though it starts off small, it grows and our faith is to be like that seed that has grown and becomes larger than all the other plants in our garden. This plant must be larger than our "TV watching plant", larger than our "worldly mindset plant", and larger than our other "plants". In fact, it is to become so big that everything else in our lives is dependent on it, like birds of the air able to make nests in its shade. If anything, our faith is to be like a solid tall oak tree, not a tiny seed! Seed is a good way to start off, but you don't leave a seed like that; you sow it. Ask any farmer if he wants just seed, or if he wants to sow that seed and reap more of the same.

GROWING THE MUSTARD SEED INTO A TREE

Like any seed, faith needs watering and feeding, as well as the right conditions for growth. Then it's all up to us how fast and how much that seed grows. Look at people in your life or in your fellowship, and tell me you can't see this comparison played out; would you not say, clearly, that some walk in more faith than others? Those strong in their faith didn't get that way overnight, trust me.

But if you and I would do the things it takes to water our faith seed with the Scriptures, with prayer, with praying in the Holy Spirit, with meditating on the things above and not on hours and hours of TV, then woe to the devil when he comes across a faithful saint who walks in this mountain-moving faith!

Back to Matthew 17:14-21. As mentioned previously, this passage shows that just because the followers of Christ — his disciples — didn't manifest the healing (initially, anyway) doesn't mean it was God's will for someone to *stay* sick.

Not only did the disciples not accomplish something they were given authority to do — but as we established, lacked faith to carry out — Jesus Himself went ahead and did it. This passage is not just an example on Jesus teaching his disciples a lesson about something, and now "watch Me do it for you". This account shows Jesus is perfectly capable of healing and performing the miraculous out of His compassion. His desire to heal is not always demonstrated properly just because of our inabilities to accomplish what He has ordained and authorized us to do.

HEALING IS NOT NECESSARILY AUTOMATIC

I dare to say that healing hardly ever happens and operates without faith being involved on someone's part — whether it be the healer or the "healee" — usually the healer though. You'll never find Jesus refusing to heal someone b/c their faith is too small to *be* healed, but He does rebuke His disciples for their faith being too small to heal others.

The only person really demonstrating "automatic" healing in the Bible is Jesus — if you could call it "automatic" healing. But even Jesus Himself prayed more than once for someone for healing before they got it. On their way to see the priest, they were healed (Luke 17:12-16). Let's not make up functions for how God operates that aren't actually in Scripture, or if they are — not to overlook other examples of healing also.

Sure, there were some who would touch the fringe of His garment and be healed (Matt 14:35-36, Mark 6:56), and the woman who touched His garment got healed of a blood discharge instantly upon touching him (Matt 9:20-22, Mark 5:25-34), but that's not the only way healing was transferred in Jesus' ministry. My motivation for mentioning that here is to give hope and encourage people not to give up so easily when it doesn't happen right away, but to persevere — such as the blind man did who saw people as trees at first, (ref Mark 8:22-25).

I can sum up for you why some people see healing when they lay hands on the sick and others don't. It's not just faith; it's tenacity. Some people persist, like Jacob did, for the blessing. Some of us just give up too quickly if we don't get results right away and not only give up, but build doctrines out of our failures like "it wasn't God's time" or "God doesn't will to heal all".

I've heard people reject the ministry of a missionary to Mexico for almost 30 years, who has seen resurrections in his ministry, because "they don't like his attitude". I think his attitude is why I trust him (I've chosen not to name the brother in Christ) — it further evidences the fact it's God working through him and not man's own ability. But I mention it because many people associate his ministry in Mexico with dead raisings and other supernatural miracles. Sure, in talking about him there almost becomes folklore and mythology in that "Chuck Norris" kind of way. But people forget the conditions and circumstances he lives in are *far* from what any of us even talking about him could relate to such as people having to bury their own dead, and not everyone can afford proper burials or for their loved ones to be taken to morgues. This is a man who's been beaten within inches of his life, stabbed, shot, etc... He's doing hard work none of us could even relate to.

There are places he goes where people just don't have funerals and life insurance coverage and things like that. But specifically, people forget that the first time he prayed for someone to be raised up, it didn't happen. Nor the second time, or the third. This happened *many* times before seeing the first one rise up. And on the occasion he saw his first dead raising, he had prayed by the body for 14 hours solid before the results came — how many of us can even spend *one* hour in personal prayer?

I know you would do it differently, of course!

Let me repeat: circumstances can destroy any sound doctrine, and most doctrines in the Body of Christ are built around failure instead of the Word of God. But how many of us are willing to persist when we lay our hands on someone and they don't immediately show results? How many of you reading will keep going for it, or will you let your "sensibilities" tell you it's foolish or that your evangelical peers will think you're a flake if you speak too much about it or go "too out there" with this stuff? Having our theological "if God wants them healed He will heal them Himself" ducks in a row more often than not is an excuse for inaction, apathy and, where applicable, outright laziness.

THE REAL REASON YOU WON'T PRAY FOR HEALING

Are you *afraid* if you go up to that person in a wheelchair you might look stupid? Trust me, you *will* look stupid, so quit worrying about it. I remember being in Charlotte, North Carolina a few years back, at Concord Mills Mall with some Bible school students. I chickened out the first two times I saw someone in a wheelchair. I made those same excuses to myself as everybody else does. But then it grated on me — "well, no guts, no glory". The third person I saw, I went up to him, and he said no. Dang. I really was in the zone too! Then it dawned on me, what's the worst that could happen? They say no if you ask? Or they don't immediately get up if they do let you pray for them?

I'd like to say on this occasion I prayed for all the wheel-chair bound people in that mall and they all got healed and we took the chairs and put them in a pickup truck to take to the dump, while revival broke out in the mall. Sorry, not on that occasion. This was earlier in my journey.

But meanwhile, on another occasion prior to that, one of the first times I ever stepped out in faith, I saw a homeless man healed of diabetes.

Allow me to finish this chapter with this: what if, in order to get the breakthrough, God told you first to pray for a thousand people who would not be healed, before you started seeing healings regularly? If you have a brain, you'll lay your hands on everything that lets you until you've reached number 1000! Then, go back to the first person and pray for them now that it's working.

"Steve, God will not allow many people to operate in healing, because it will cause people to fall into pride."

Right, like you've never been in pride before! And God

would keep somebody sick in order to avoid having you fall into pride? *That* is pride already!

Trust me, there is *no* reason for anyone not to go for it. We just make all the excuses in the world out of fear of failure, fear of rejection on the part of the person we seek to heal and fear of taking responsibility for a miracle God enabled believers to do.

You'll never know now will you if you don't go for it

LIE #6: I DIDN'T GET HEALED THE FIRST TIME I PRAYED, SO IT MUST NOT BE GOD'S WILL TO HEAL ME"

IN MATTHEW 17:14-21, as mentioned in the previous lie, the disciples were unable to heal a boy with epilepsy, and then Jesus went ahead and prayed for the boy and he was healed instantly. This passage also shows that just because healing didn't happen doesn't mean it was God's will for someone to stay sick. His desire to heal is not always demonstrated properly just because of our inabilities to accomplish what He has ordained and authorized us to do.

The disciples prayed, and the boy wasn't healed. Jesus then prayed, which would be at least the second time the boy received prayer, and then he received his healing. It was no less God's will to heal the boy when the disciples were praying for him than it was when Jesus Himself prayed for the boy.

Ergo, the amount of times we pray for healing does not reveal or indicate God's will in someone's sickness or illness — the Word of God does.

Take note of the following account:

> "And He took the blind man by the hand and led him out of the village, and when He had spit on his eyes and laid his hands on him, He asked him, "Do you see anything?" And he looked up and said, "I see men, but they look like trees, walking." Then Jesus **laid His hands on his eyes again**; and he opened his eyes, his sight was restored, and he saw everything clearly." (Mark 8:23-25, emphasis mine)

Philippians 2:6-8 states that Jesus, co-equal with God, didn't consider Himself as God when He lived on the earth. He operated as an anointed man.

Even Christ Himself — God in man, remember — prayed more than once for someone to be healed before they obtained it. We observe in this passage of Scripture that he took the man by the hand, spat on his eyes (I'd love to see a healing evangelist do this in person) and laid his hands on him. At this point the man still wasn't seeing people clearly.

It was the second time the Son of God prayed that improvement was obvious.

My personal experience resembles the above a lot more than instantaneous healing, in that often I pray several times for someone, or have had to persist for quite some time in praying for someone to be healed.

We could also include in this particular lie the truth that very often healing is not instantaneous like people believe, but requires perseverance.

Let's say that you didn't get healed on the first try. Instead, you got healed on the 10th time. I've heard Rev. Curry Blake liken it to medicine — each time you received prayer was one tenth of your healing and then finally on the tenth prayer, you were full and got healed. This is not a perfect analogy, but it helps us understand that we may not have all the answers as to why a healing seemed to take a while. But the fact of the matter is it can require praying more than once.

I also heard Blake share anecdotally in a meeting that the students in John G. Lake's healing rooms ministry would pray for someone every day for however long it took until they were healed. Graduating the divine healing technician training was dependent on them being able to actually produce results — healed individuals.

There's precedent for the idea of needing to persevere sometimes before seeing the healing take place. Ideally instantaneous healing is preferable, but we need to cut ourselves some slack when it's not a life and death situation and realize that it can be a process. Our prayers can sometimes be acting as fertilizer to prepare the soil of our own hearts to receive the miracle.

In the eleventh chapter of Mark, when Jesus had entered Jerusalem, there's a familiar passage of Scripture that I want you to draw hope from, about the fig tree:

> On the following day, when they came from Bethany, He was hungry. And seeing in the distance a fig tree in leaf, He went to see if he could find anything on it. When He came to it, He found nothing but leaves, for it was not the season for figs. And He said to it, "May no one ever eat fruit from you again." And his disciples heard it. (vv 12-14)

First of all, notice that in Mark's account, Jesus cursed the fig tree here and then kept walking on his way to the temple which He then cleansed. Afterward, according to verse 20, they passed by the fig tree the *next* morning and saw the results of the word Jesus spoke the day before. He didn't lay a hand on it and proclaim a lightning bolt to zap it. He cursed it with His words.

There's the power of life and death in the tongue, and we can use it for blessing or cursing (James 3:9-11). This is an example of it being used this way.

Lack of instantaneous results can discourage us into believing nothing has happened. However, we need to remember something: the fig tree didn't demonstrate any discernible evidence that it had been cursed and no longer bearing fruit.

According to Mark's gospel account, it may not have been noticeable until a day later.

Sometimes speaking the Word of God over our circumstances doesn't yield a noticeable result right away, but in the Spirit the prayer has been answered and the outward circumstances are already in the process of changing.

Maybe the cancer in that person's body has been removed, and now the body needs normal healing to recuperate from all the damage that the curse has caused. We walk by faith and not by sight, and sometimes appearances don't tell the whole story. Like the fig tree, the roots of a problem can be dealt with but the branches don't look dead right away.

Maybe you aren't needing healing in your body, but you pray for people and feel like you're not seeing any results. Keep this principle in your mind, and by faith, keep praying for people and don't let circumstances deter you.

As I mentioned in the previous chapter about praying for

1000 people before finally seeing results and then going back and praying for person number 1 again, I encourage you to go do the same if you find yourself in this situation.

A sure-fire way to make sure you don't see any results is to not even try.

CONCLUDING THOUGHTS

IF YOU MADE it this far, I want to thank you. If you grew up viewing God as some cop in the sky looking for ways to punish you every time you did wrong, or that sickness and diseases are "blessings" from Him we should never give back, then I thank you for plowing through all this stuff that contradicts that. It's not easy to find out things we believed to be the truth were actually lies. But it's my hope and prayer that this little book didn't just demolish those lies, but helps to give you encouragement and hope.

My intention when putting this together was to focus more on debunking the myths Christians typically believe about God which hinder their healing. In fact, I almost wrote a chapter on the lie that there's a hindrance to healing, but decided to leave this as a short book that could be read in a few hours.

In our missional community here in Peru, we're in the habit of asking people in every one of our house meetings if they need healing in their bodies. Whenever someone raises their hand or comes forward, we ask someone else in the meeting to do the honors of laying hands on them. The reason for this is so that we don't accidentally reenforce the lie that only special anointed ministers are the ones who can heal the sick, but that if someone has the Holy Spirit in them, they have same Spirit that raised Jesus from the dead. We reinforce that it's not us who do anything.

That being said, I hope you are able to put this book down with confidence and go forward knowing you carry that same anointing to lay hands on the sick. If you'd like to study this more or go further into healing beyond just having changed your mind about certain Scriptures and doctrines about God's will to heal, then please check out the resources at the end of this book.

RESOURCES

THIS BOOK WAS INTENDED to be a gateway or
introduction to this subject to help you clear up the
common misconceptions about divine healing that many
struggle with.

If you'd like to read more in depth, the following are the
best resources to use in my estimation, and some of which
I used for reference in preparing this book.

BOOKS:

*John G Lake – The Complete Collection of His Life
Teachings* compiled by Roberts Liardon

God's Covenant of Healing – SJ Hill

God's Will Is Always Healing: Crushing Theological Barriers to Healing - by Joshua Greeson

Divine Healing Made Simple - by Praying Medic

Healing the Sick — T.L. Osborn

Christ The Healer — F.F. Bosworth

AUDIO TEACHINGS:

Recommended Fire On Your Head Podcast episodes:

How To Receive From God — A podcast discussion between the author, Joel Crumpton and Brian Parkman.

Faith and Healing — A 90 minute teaching by the author from the *Fire For Life Summer School* in The Netherlands in 2007

Interview with Joshua Greeson, author of *God's Will Is Always Healing*

Why Don't Some People Get Healed? &

Is Taking Medicine a Sign of Unbelief? Two-part discussions with Praying Medic, author of *Divine Healing Made Simple*

Do You Have a Thorn in the Flesh? Interview with Art Thomas, director of *Paid in Full* documentary

ABOUT THE AUTHOR

STEVE BREMNER IS a missionary to Peru and a *FIRE School of Ministry* graduate. He has a burden for grounding people in the Word of God and seeing believers from all sorts of backgrounds live out and experience the power of the Holy Spirit, and the love of God in their lives and ministries.

Steve also thinks it's pretentious when authors and bloggers write their own bio pages but refer to themselves in the third person.

I — I mean *he* — served in the Netherlands for almost 2 years before moving to South America. The gift of teaching and a pastoral heart are what characterize Steve's calling, and in Peru so far he's had opportunities to teach in a local seminary, share the love of Christ to some of the underprivileged, and traveled to shanty towns outside of Lima, the nation's capital, to teach with and serve alongside other established ministries. He is now living in Chorrillos, and is part of a missional community called *Oikos,* and teaches full time in its school of ministry.

Steve is Canadian (and is not ashamed of it), and was sent out by *River Run Fellowship,* located in Peterborough, Ontario. That's in Canada, for those who need it clarified. If it weren't for his home fellowship, and its lead elder Stephen Best, he would never have gone to Peru where he is beginning to see God do things he once only imagined and daydreamed about.

Like any other author, Steve and Lili are using the proceeds from their online book sales to finance their disciple-making in Peru. One way you can support them that doesn't require any of your money is by leaving a rating and writing a review of this book on sites where it can be downloaded.

IF THE INTERNET had been available to the Apostle Paul, he'd have used it make the Word of God available to as many people as he could. For this reason, Steve co-hosts and produces the *Fire On Your Head* podcast, which can be subscribed to in iTunes and other popular podcatcher programs such as Stitcher Radio and Google Play Music Podcasts.

You can visit the site directly at
www.fireonyourhead.com.

INCREASE YOUR FAITH

Practical Steps To Help You Believe For The Impossible

Have you ever wondered what Jesus was talking about when he told us we could cast mountains into the sea? Have you ever wondered the point of having faith like a mustard seed?

Hebrews 11:6 says that without faith it is impossible to please God, but yet so many of us have little idea what this means exactly. Jesus said if we had faith as a mustard seed, we could speak to our mountainous problems and cast them into the sea.

Loaded with Scripture, this quick read contains practical

tips that you can immediately apply to your personal life, and start casting your mountains into the sea!

Increase Your Faith was written to provide you with spiritual guidance and usable insights to help you see the impossible come about in your life.

GET THESE BONUSES WHEN YOU BUY OUR AUDIOBOOK

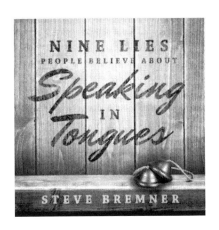

9 LIES PEOPLE BELIEVE ABOUT SPEAKING IN TONGUES IS FINALLY AVAILABLE IN AUDIO BOOK FORMAT

HAVE you ever been told that speaking in tongues is "not for today?"

Maybe you've heard people speak in tongues... and it seemed weird. You thought to yourself, *"This is too strange to be God!"*

Or, maybe you believe that people can still speak in tongues today... but it's not for everybody.

Whether you're skeptical or intrigued, whether you speak in tongues or don't, this book is for you!

In Nine Lies People Believe About Speaking in Tongues, I biblically confront myths about speaking in tongues head-on and answer some of the most common questions about this controversial spiritual gift.

But wait — there's more!

If you buy a copy of the audio book on Audible, Amazon, iTunes or wherever you can *legitimately* get it, I'll send you 7 bonus mp3s from Brian Parkman, mentor of mine and co-writer of two of the chapters. These files he's given me permission to give away are teachings he offered in recent years on the following:

- **2 classes** of *The More Excellent Way* (see 1 Corinthians 13)
- **5 classes** of *Practicing and Imparting Spirit Baptism*

Each class on average is between 60-75 minutes long,

making this upwards of 7 hours of bonus content, and perfect for those of you wanting to understand the dynamics of the various types of the gift of speaking in tongues. You'll also learn to minister the baptism to other people and help them understand it better, along with other really cool stuff that has personally had a big impact on me and my relationship with the Holy Spirit.

All of this for only $14.95 (or $9.95 if you're already an AudibleListener) and if you read to the end I'll tell you how to **get it free**!

WHY AUDIO?

I know you're a smart cookie who knows how to read. You got this far didn't you? Audio means you can learn on the go. While driving or commuting, working out at the gym or while doing chores like giving your dog a bath. There have been studies that have shown that we need to *hear* **something at least three times before we can really grab hold** and run with the information. Reading works too, but how many of us will read a book three times? Listening three times is a breeze. When you lead someone into a Holy Spirit baptism, you need the "how" engrained. You need to not be flipping through a book looking up the info.

SOUND GOOD? OK, HERE'S HOW YOU GET IT!

If you purchase the audio book from audibletrial.com/fire-onyourhead and forward me your receipt or your order confirmation — anything digital or scanned proving you legitimately got the audio book — to **fireonyourhead (AT) stevebremner (DOT) com**, I'll personally send you a link with all the bonus downloads.

If you join Audible's 30 day trial, you'll be given a credit that can be used toward the book allowing you to get it for free. You can forward me your order confirmation even if you didn't pay for the book but simply used the free credit you got with your 30 day free trial.

If you already have the Kindle version or you want to read it as well, you can get the Audible Narration added for only $7.49 as well. When buying the Kindle book on Amazon, you'll see the option to add Audible narration when purchasing the book.

That Audible membership will be a handy time saver for all of the things you want to learn, although you can cancel your membership when your 30 days are up and still keep the audiobook long after.

RULES/TERMS/CONDITIONS/THE FINE
PRINT/THINGS YOU SHOULD KNOW

- I check this email account once every 24 hours daily. Please be patient if you don't hear from me immediately.
- Prices presented to you by Audible or Amazon may be different from listener to listener, based on various things such as whether you're already an AudibleListener or a new one, and geographical location while browsing the web.
- You CAN purchase the book on Amazon or iTunes and forward me that receipt. However, you will only be able to start a free 30 day trial (and obtain the audiobook free) on Audible.

PARTNER WITH US AS
MISSIONARIES

IF YOU WERE TOUCHED by this book and would like to make a donation to sow directly into Steve and Lili Bremner on the mission field in Peru, please follow these instructions:

IN THE USA:

Make checks payable to:

WORLD OUTREACH CENTER

PO Box 3478,

Fort Mill, SC 29708

Please Indicate it's for The Bremners /Peru

Visit their site to donate online:
www.worldoutreachcommunity.org

Thank you for your encouragement and support.

Made in the USA
Columbia, SC
20 February 2019